FRIDAY

IS

FISH

and Shrimp and Scallops and Crab and More

◆ ◆ ◆

TIME-LIFE BOOKS, ALEXANDRIA, VIRGINIA

TIME-LIFE BOOKS IS A DIVISION OF TIME LIFE INC.

PRESIDENT and CEO, Time Life Inc. — John M. Fahey Jr.
PRESIDENT, Time-Life Books — John D. Hall

TIME-LIFE CUSTOM PUBLISHING

VICE PRESIDENT and PUBLISHER — Terry Newell
Director of Sales — Neil Levin
Director of New Product Development — Regina Hall
Managing Editor — Donia Ann Steele
Editorial Director — Jennifer Pearce
Senior Art Director — Christopher M. Register
Sales Manager — Liz Ziehl
Retail Promotions Manager — Gary Stoiber
Associate Marketing Manager — Dana A. Coleman
Operations Manager — Valerie Lewis
Director of Financial Operations — J. Brian Birky
Financial Analyst — Trish Palini
Production Manager — Carolyn Bounds
Quality Assurance Manager — Miriam P. Newton
Executive Assistant — Tammy York

Produced by Rebus, Inc.
New York, New York

Illustrations
William Neeper

Library of Congress Cataloging-in-Publication Data
Friday is fish and shrimp and scallops and crab and more.
p. cm. -- (The Everyday cookbooks)
Includes index.
ISBN 0-8094-9190-7
ISBN 0-7835-4779-4
1. Cookery (Fish) 2. Cookery (Shellfish) 3. Quick and easy cookery.
I. Time-Life Books. II. Series.
TX747.F728   1995
641.6'92--dc20

95-18647
CIP

Introduction

Remember when you could tell what day of the week it was by what Mom was making for dinner? It was predictable, and comforting, and—as far as Mom was concerned—efficient. But every now and then, didn't you wish she would give her usual tuna casserole recipe a rest and try something new? Now here's a cookbook that not only helps you plan meals like Mom used to make but gives you a wonderful variety of recipes, too. With *Friday Is Fish,* you can offer your family a delightfully different seafood meal every week.

To make life even easier, this cookbook includes the following features:

- There are no difficult techniques or exotic ingredients. All of the recipes can be made with supermarket-available foods, and a great many of them can be made entirely with ingredients already in the pantry.

- Each recipe is designed with everyone's busy schedule in mind, with most taking under 30 minutes to prepare. These recipes are labeled "Extra-Quick" and are marked with this symbol: ◆ (A full listing of the extra-quick recipes is included in the index under the heading Extra-Quick.)

- Many of the recipes include lower-fat alternatives, such as reduced-fat sour cream and low-fat milk. In addition, we have created a number of recipes that get fewer than 30 percent of their calories from fat. These recipes are labeled "Low-Fat" and are marked with this symbol: ◇ (A full listing of the low-fat recipes is included in the index under the heading Low-Fat.)

- As a further help to the cook, there are notes throughout the book that provide simple variations on recipes, cooking shortcuts or tips on how to lower fat, suggestions for simple desserts that can be made for weekday meals, and substitutions, in case you can't find (or don't like) certain ingredients.

- In a special section called "Family Favorites," we include recipes that even the pickiest eaters will like, such as Garlic-Lemon Shrimp and Crispy Flounder with Sweet-and-Sour Sauce.

But best of all, in *Friday Is Fish* there are enough delicious seafood recipes for more than two years' worth of Fridays!

CONTENTS

SOUPS AND CHOWDERS

Fish Soup with Vegetables and Red Pepper Sauce 6

Seafood Soup Provençale 7

Savory Clam and Rice Soup 8

Scallop-Mushroom Noodle Soup 9

Spicy Shrimp and Spinach Soup 10

Corn, Scallop, and Fettuccine Soup 11

Fast Fish Chowder 12

Salmon and Corn Chowder 13

Rich Red Snapper Chowder with Carrots 14

New England Fish Chowder 15

Tomato-Clam Chowder with Garlic Toasts 16

Boston Crab Chowder with Nutmeg Croutons 17

BRAISES AND STEWS

Italian-Style Fish Fillets 18

Fish Curry with Spinach and Peanuts 19

Spicy Fish Ragout over Lemon Rice 20

Curried Flounder with Mushrooms 21

Caribbean Red Snapper Stew 22

Seafood Stew with Water Chestnuts 23

Cod Stewed with Potatoes, Corn, and Tomatoes 24

Quick Cioppino with Parsley Toasts 25

Blackened Seafood Stew 26

New Orleans Fish and Oyster Stew 27

Ragout of Scallops and Red Peppers 28

Creole-Style Scallops and Rice 29

Mexican-Style Shrimp with Pasta and Tomatoes 30

Shrimp Curry with Coconut-Almond Rice 31

Shrimp with Green Chili Creole Sauce 32

STEAMED AND POACHED

Oriental Oven-Steamed Fish with Vegetables 33

Steamed Fish with Ginger, Scallions, and Cilantro 34

Chinese-Style Poached Fish Fillets 35

Fillets of Flounder Capri 36

Cod Basque-Style 37

Poached Salmon in Orange-Lemon Sauce 38

Red Snapper with Vegetable Julienne 39

Poached Salmon with Dill Butter 40

Salmon with Dill Sauce 41

Tex-Mex Steamed Swordfish 42

Swordfish and Leeks with Bell Pepper Purée 43

PAN-FRIES

Pan-Fried Halibut with Sweet-and-Sour Sauce 44

Breaded Fish with Lemon Butter 45

Sautéed Sesame Fish 46

Shallow-Fried Fish Tempura with Two Sauces 47

Sautéed Curried Grouper 48

Pan-Fried Haddock with Spanish Vegetables 49

Monkfish Provençale 50

Salmon Patties with Citrus Vinaigrette 51

Salmon with Fresh Basil Sauce 52

Corn-Fried Snapper with Spicy Pineapple Salsa 53

Pecan-Crusted Snapper with Scallions 54

Red Snapper with Toasted Almonds 55

Red Snapper with Spicy Orange Sauce 56

Mexican-Style Sole with Almonds 57

Sole with Tomato-Basil Sauce 58

Brook Trout with Mushroom Sauce 59

Swordfish Piccata 60

Crab Cakes with Quick Rémoulade Sauce 61

Lemon Scallops with Green Beans 62

Scallop-Asparagus Stir-Fry with Curried Rice 63

Spicy Shrimp on Zucchini Nests 64

Lemon-Garlic Shrimp with Parslied Rice 65

Sautéed Shrimp with Sherry and Chilies 66

Garlic Shrimp with Cuban Black Bean Salad 67

Baked Dishes

Baked Tarragon Fish 68

Codfish Cakes with Horseradish Sauce 69

Flounder Rolls Stuffed with Cheese and Spinach 70

Baked Cod with Tomatoes and Provolone 71

Fillets of Flounder Sorrento 72

Shrimp-Stuffed Baked Fish 73

Greek-Style Baked Haddock 74

Skillet-Baked Flounder Provençale 75

Mushroom-Smothered Baked Fish 76

Buttermilk Baked Halibut 77

Sole Baked in Parchment 78

Fillets of Sole in Wine Sauce 79

Baked Sole with Mushrooms and Tomatoes 80

Baked Sole with Zucchini and Peppers 81

Foil-Baked Sole and Vegetables with Herb Butter 82

Bourbon-Basted Salmon 83

Herb-Coated Salmon 84

Baked Red Snapper with Chili Sauce 85

Skillet-Baked Trout with Lemon-Caper Sauce 86

Striped Bass with Fennel and Romaine 87

Tuna Baked in Parchment with Red Peppers 88

Baked Stuffed Shrimp with Tomato Tartar Sauce 89

Grilled and Broiled

Flounder with Lemon Cream 90

Lime-Dressed Snapper with Potatoes and Peppers 91

Broiled Scrod with Red Pepper Butter 92

Marinated Red Snapper 93

Cod Steaks Topped with Tomato and Basil 94

Grilled Salmon Steaks with Fresh Dill and Thyme 95

Broiled Salmon with Green Sauce 96

Lemon-Marinated Swordfish Kebabs 97

Swordfish with Spicy Tomato-Orange Sauce 98

Broiled Tuna with Orange-Cumin Sauce 99

Scallop and Vegetable Skewers with Garlic Butter 100

Grilled Shrimp with Tomato-Ginger Sauce 101

Broiled Shrimp with Cilantro-Citrus Butter 102

Broiled Crab-Potato Patties 103

Salads

Grilled Fish Salad 104

Salmon-Rice Salad with Lemon-Pepper Dressing 105

Zesty Tuna with Mexican Seasonings 106

Tuna-Spinach Salad with Peanut Dressing 107

Tuna Salad Niçoise 108

Shrimp and Green Bean Salad 109

Asian Crab-and-Vegetable Salad 110

Family Favorites

Mixed Seafood Chowder 111

Light Seafood Newburg 112

Mussels Marinière 113

Steamed Spiced Crabs 114

Pan-Blackened Red Snapper 115

Beer Batter Fillets with Red Pepper Slaw 116

Chili Shrimp 117

Tuna Burgers 118

Crispy Flounder with Sweet-and-Sour Sauce 119

Broiled Sole with Garlic Butter and Bread Crumbs 120

Spicy Broiled Salmon 121

Broiled Swordfish with Herb Butter 122

Parmesan Scallop Gratin 123

Garlic-Lemon Shrimp 124

Paella Salad 125

Index

Index 126

FISH SOUP WITH VEGETABLES AND RED PEPPER SAUCE

SERVES 4

2 WHOLE WHEAT BREAD SLICES, CRUSTS REMOVED

6 CUPS FISH BROTH, BOTTLED CLAM JUICE, OR REDUCED-SODIUM CHICKEN BROTH

1 MEDIUM RED BELL PEPPER, COARSELY CHOPPED

2 LARGE GARLIC CLOVES, CHOPPED

⅛ TEASPOON CAYENNE PEPPER

3 TABLESPOONS OLIVE OIL

3 LARGE LEEKS, WHITE PARTS ONLY, THINLY SLICED

3 CUPS FINELY SHREDDED SAVOY CABBAGE

2 TOMATOES, CHOPPED

1 POUND COD, HADDOCK, OR OCEAN PERCH FILLETS, CUT INTO 1-INCH CHUNKS

¼ CUP GRATED ROMANO CHEESE

1. In a shallow bowl, combine the bread slices and enough water to cover. Set aside to soak for 10 minutes.

2. Meanwhile, in a large saucepan, bring the broth to a boil.

3. Squeeze out the water from the bread and transfer the bread to a food processor. Add the bell pepper, garlic, and cayenne, and purée the mixture until smooth. With the machine still running, dribble in the oil; the resulting sauce should be thick. Set the sauce aside.

4. Add the leeks, cabbage, and tomatoes to the boiling broth, reduce the heat to low, and simmer the vegetables until they are tender, about 10 minutes.

5. Add the fish, cover, and cook until the fish is just firm and opaque, about 3 minutes. Pass the cheese and the red pepper sauce in separate bowls to spoon on top of the soup.

SEAFOOD SOUP PROVENÇALE

SERVES 4

¼ CUP OLIVE OIL

3 LARGE CARROTS, THINLY SLICED

1 LARGE ONION, HALVED AND THINLY
   SLICED

2 CELERY RIBS, THINLY SLICED

1¾ CUPS DRY WHITE WINE

2 TABLESPOONS PERNOD (OPTIONAL)

ONE 16-OUNCE CAN NO-SALT-ADDED
   WHOLE TOMATOES

1 BAY LEAF

¼ TEASPOON SALT

¼ TEASPOON BLACK PEPPER

12 MEDIUM SHRIMP, SHELLED AND
   DEVEINED

12 LITTLENECK CLAMS OR MUSSELS,
   SCRUBBED

1 POUND COD, HALIBUT, OR SEA BASS
   FILLETS, CUT INTO 1½-INCH
   SQUARES

1. In a large saucepan, warm the oil over medium-high heat. Reduce the heat to medium. Add the carrots, onion, and celery, and sauté, stirring frequently, until the carrots and celery are bright in color, 2 to 3 minutes.

2. Add the wine and Pernod (if using), increase the heat to medium-high, and cook for 3 minutes.

3. Add the tomatoes, bay leaf, salt, and pepper, and break up the tomatoes with the back of a spoon. Bring to a boil, reduce the heat to low, and simmer, stirring occasionally, for 5 minutes.

4. Add the shrimp and clams, and simmer for 3 minutes.

5. Add the fish and simmer just until the fish and shrimp are opaque and the clams open, about 5 minutes. Discard any clams that remain closed. Remove and discard the bay leaf before serving.

SAVORY CLAM AND RICE SOUP

SERVES 4

◇ LOW-FAT

2 DOZEN LITTLENECK CLAMS,
   SCRUBBED

1 TABLESPOON OLIVE OIL

½ CUP MINCED ONION

2 TEASPOONS MINCED GARLIC

1 SMALL BAY LEAF

¼ CUP RICE

¼ CUP DRY WHITE WINE

⅛ TEASPOON CRUSHED SAFFRON
   THREADS (OPTIONAL)

½ TEASPOON FRESH LEMON JUICE

1 LARGE TOMATO, FINELY CHOPPED

2 TABLESPOONS CHOPPED PARSLEY

1. In a large pot, bring 4 cups of water to a boil over high heat. Add the clams, cover the pot tightly, and cook the clams until they open, about 5 minutes. Transfer the clams to a plate, discarding any that remain closed, and reserve the cooking liquid. When the clams are cool enough to handle, remove them from their shells. Discard the shells and set the clams aside.

2. In a large skillet, warm the oil over medium heat. Add the onion, garlic, and bay leaf, and sauté, stirring frequently, until the onion is translucent, about 5 minutes.

3. Strain the reserved clam cooking liquid through a sieve lined with cheesecloth, then pour the liquid back into the pot. Add the contents of the skillet along with the rice, wine, saffron (if using), and lemon juice, and bring the mixture to a boil. Reduce the heat to low, partially cover the pot, and simmer the mixture for 10 minutes, stirring once or twice.

4. Add the tomato and simmer, uncovered, for 5 minutes. Stir in the parsley and simmer for 2 minutes. Return the clams to the pot and cook just until they are heated through, 1 to 2 minutes. Remove and discard the bay leaf before serving.

Scallop-Mushroom Noodle Soup

SERVES 4

♦ EXTRA-QUICK ◇ LOW-FAT

4 CUPS REDUCED-SODIUM CHICKEN
  BROTH
3 QUARTER-SIZE SLICES FRESH GINGER,
  MINCED
1 TEASPOON ORIENTAL (DARK) SESAME
  OIL
¼ TEASPOON RED PEPPER FLAKES
¼ POUND ANGEL HAIR PASTA OR
  VERMICELLI

½ POUND SEA SCALLOPS, QUARTERED
¼ POUND BEAN SPROUTS
¼ POUND SNOW PEAS
¼ POUND MUSHROOMS, THINLY SLICED
3 SCALLIONS, CUT INTO 1½-INCH-
  LONG SLIVERS

1. In a large saucepan, bring the broth, ginger, sesame oil, and red pepper flakes to a boil over medium-high heat.

2. Meanwhile, in a large pot of boiling water, cook the pasta until al dente according to package directions.

3. Add the scallops, bean sprouts, snow peas, and mushrooms to the boiling broth mixture.

Reduce the heat to low, cover, and cook until the scallops are just opaque and the vegetables are crisp-tender, 1 to 2 minutes. Add the scallions and cook for 30 seconds.

4. Drain the pasta and divide it among 4 soup bowls. Ladle the scallop-vegetable mixture and broth on top, and serve hot.

Variation: *If you can get bay scallops, use them whole instead of the quartered sea scallops. Bay scallops are about one-third the size of sea scallops; they're sweeter, but also pricier.*

Spicy Shrimp and Spinach Soup

SERVES 4

3 TABLESPOONS UNSALTED BUTTER

1 TO 2 PICKLED JALAPEÑO PEPPERS, SEEDED AND MINCED

2 MEDIUM ONIONS, COARSELY CHOPPED

3 LARGE GARLIC CLOVES, MINCED

¾ TEASPOON OREGANO

½ TEASPOON THYME

1 BAY LEAF

2½ CUPS REDUCED-SODIUM CHICKEN BROTH

2½ CUPS FISH BROTH OR BOTTLED CLAM JUICE

1 SMALL AVOCADO

2 TABLESPOONS FRESH LIME JUICE

1 POUND MEDIUM SHRIMP, IN THE SHELL

4 CUPS (PACKED) SPINACH LEAVES, TORN INTO BITE-SIZE PIECES

¼ TEASPOON SALT

¼ TEASPOON WHITE PEPPER

1 CUP CHOPPED CILANTRO

½ CUP CHOPPED SCALLIONS

½ CUP GRATED PARMESAN CHEESE

2 SMALL LIMES, CUT INTO WEDGES

1. In a large skillet, warm the butter over medium heat until melted. Add the jalapeños, onions, and garlic, and cook, stirring frequently, until the onions are translucent, about 3 minutes. Remove the pan from the heat. Stir in the oregano, thyme, and bay leaf.

2. In a medium saucepan, bring the chicken broth and fish broth to a boil over high heat. Add the sautéed vegetables and return to a boil. Reduce the heat to low and simmer for 30 minutes.

3. Meanwhile, halve and peel the avocado. Remove and discard the pit. Cut the flesh into

½-inch dice. In a small bowl, toss the avocado with 1 tablespoon of the lime juice. Set aside.

4. Increase the heat under the broth to high and return to a boil. Add the shrimp and cook just until they are firm and the shells turn bright pink, about 3 minutes.

5. Turn off the heat under the shrimp. Stir in the spinach and the remaining 1 tablespoon lime juice, cover, and allow to steam for 2 minutes. Season with the salt and pepper.

6. Serve the soup with the avocado, cilantro, scallions, Parmesan, and lime wedges.

Corn, Scallop, and Fettuccine Soup

SERVES 4

◆ EXTRA-QUICK ◇ LOW-FAT

¾ POUND SEA SCALLOPS, HALVED IF
    LARGE

½ TEASPOON SALT

⅛ TEASPOON WHITE PEPPER

4 CUPS FISH BROTH, BOTTLED CLAM
    JUICE, OR REDUCED-SODIUM
    CHICKEN BROTH

1 CUP LOW-FAT MILK

¼ POUND SPINACH FETTUCCINE

⅔ CUP FRESH OR FROZEN CORN
    KERNELS

1 TABLESPOON OLIVE OIL

1 TABLESPOON UNSALTED BUTTER

2 TABLESPOONS FINELY CHOPPED
    SHALLOT OR ONION

½ CUP DRY WHITE WINE

½ TEASPOON CHOPPED FRESH THYME,
    OR ¼ TEASPOON DRIED

1. Season the scallops with ¼ teaspoon of the salt and the pepper, and set them aside.

2. In a large pot, combine the broth, milk, and the remaining ¼ teaspoon salt. Bring the mixture to a boil and add the fettuccine and corn. Cover the pot until the liquid returns to a boil, then cook, uncovered, until the pasta is al dente, about 8 minutes.

3. Meanwhile, in a large skillet, warm the oil with the butter over medium-high heat until

the butter is melted. Add the scallops and sauté them for 30 seconds on each side. Add the shallot and cook, stirring constantly, for 1 minute. Pour in the wine, then add the thyme and cook, stirring, for 1 minute.

4. Remove the broth mixture from the heat, add the scallop mixture, and stir well to combine. Serve the soup hot.

FAST FISH CHOWDER

SERVES 4

◆ EXTRA-QUICK ◇ LOW-FAT

2¾ CUPS REDUCED-SODIUM CHICKEN
    BROTH
1 POUND ALL-PURPOSE POTATOES,
    PEELED AND CUT INTO ½-INCH DICE
1 MEDIUM ONION, COARSELY CHOPPED
½ POUND SCROD, COD, OR HADDOCK
    FILLETS

2 MEDIUM CARROTS, CUT INTO
    ½-INCH DICE
2 CELERY RIBS, CUT INTO ½-INCH DICE
½ TEASPOON SALT
¼ TEASPOON BLACK PEPPER
1 CUP LOW-FAT MILK

1. In a large saucepan, bring the broth to a boil over medium-high heat. Add the potatoes and onion, reduce the heat to medium-low, cover, and simmer, stirring occasionally, until the potatoes are tender, about 15 minutes.

2. Meanwhile, cut the fish into ¾-inch cubes.

3. Increase the heat under the potatoes to medium-high and return the liquid to a boil. Add the fish, carrots, celery, salt, and pepper.

4. Reduce the heat to medium-low, cover the pan, and simmer until the fish just flakes when tested with a fork, 5 to 7 minutes.

5. Stir in the milk and cook, stirring, just until heated through, 1 to 2 minutes.

KITCHEN NOTE: *The fish sold as scrod is simply a small, young cod or haddock. Be sure to get fillets that are at least ¾ inch thick so you can cut the fish into generous cubes.*

Salmon and Corn Chowder

SERVES 4

◇ LOW-FAT

3 SLICES OF BACON, CUT CROSSWISE
  INTO THIN STRIPS
1 MEDIUM ONION, COARSELY CHOPPED
2 GARLIC CLOVES, MINCED
2 TABLESPOONS FLOUR
2½ CUPS REDUCED-SODIUM CHICKEN
  BROTH
1 POUND UNPEELED RED POTATOES,
  CUT INTO ½-INCH CUBES

1 MEDIUM GREEN BELL PEPPER, DICED
2 CUPS FROZEN CORN, THAWED
¼ TEASPOON BLACK PEPPER
½ POUND SALMON FILLET, CUT INTO
  ½-INCH CUBES
1 CUP LOW-FAT MILK
¼ CUP (PACKED) FRESH DILL SPRIGS,
  MINCED, OR 2 TEASPOONS DRIED

1. In a medium saucepan, cook the bacon over medium heat, stirring frequently, until crisp, about 10 minutes. Drain the bacon on paper towels and set aside. Pour off all but 1 tablespoon of fat from the pan.

2. Add the onion and garlic to the pan and cook over medium-high heat, stirring frequently, until the onion begins to brown, about 5 minutes.

3. Stir in the flour and cook, stirring constantly, until the flour is no longer visible, about 30 seconds. Add the broth and potatoes, and bring to a boil. Reduce the heat to medium-low, cover, and simmer until the potatoes are tender, about 15 minutes.

4. Return the broth mixture to a boil over medium-high heat. Add the bell pepper, corn, and black pepper, and cook until the bell pepper is crisp-tender, about 5 minutes.

5. Transfer about half of the mixture to a food processor and purée until smooth, then return the purée to the saucepan. Return the mixture to a simmer over medium-low heat, add the salmon and milk, and cook until the salmon flakes easily, 3 to 5 minutes.

6. Remove the pan from the heat and stir in the dill. Serve the chowder garnished with the bacon.

RICH RED SNAPPER
CHOWDER WITH CARROTS

SERVES 4

⅓ CUP FLOUR

⅜ TEASPOON BLACK PEPPER

1 POUND RED SNAPPER OR GROUPER
FILLETS, CUT INTO 1-INCH CHUNKS

2 TABLESPOONS OLIVE OIL

1 TABLESPOON UNSALTED BUTTER

2 CUPS REDUCED-SODIUM CHICKEN
BROTH

1½ TEASPOONS THYME

PINCH OF CAYENNE PEPPER

4 MEDIUM CARROTS, COARSELY
CHOPPED

4 CELERY RIBS, COARSELY CHOPPED

¼ CUP CHOPPED PARSLEY (OPTIONAL)

1. In a shallow bowl, combine the flour and ⅛ teaspoon of the pepper. Dredge the fish lightly in the seasoned flour, reserving the excess seasoned flour.

2. In a large nonstick skillet, warm 1 tablespoon of the oil with the butter over medium-high heat until the butter is melted. Add the fish and cook until golden brown all over, about 7 minutes. Be careful when turning the fish to keep the pieces intact. Transfer the fish to a plate and cover loosely with foil to keep warm.

3. Add the remaining 1 tablespoon oil to the skillet and warm over medium heat. Stir in the reserved seasoned flour and cook, stirring

constantly, until the flour is dark brown, 4 to 5 minutes.

4. Gradually add the broth to the flour, stirring constantly to keep the mixture smooth. Stir in the thyme, cayenne, and the remaining ¼ teaspoon black pepper.

5. Increase the heat to medium-high and bring the mixture to a boil. Add the carrots, celery, and parsley (if using), reduce the heat to low, cover, and simmer until the vegetables are tender, about 5 minutes.

6. Add the cooked fish to the chowder, stir gently, and cook, uncovered, until the fish is heated through, about 2 minutes.

New England Fish Chowder

SERVES 4

½ POUND BACON, CUT CROSSWISE
  INTO THIN STRIPS
2 TABLESPOONS UNSALTED BUTTER
2 LARGE ONIONS, SLICED
¼ TEASPOON SALT
¼ TEASPOON BLACK PEPPER
¼ TEASPOON THYME
1 LARGE BAKING POTATO, PEELED AND
  CUT INTO ½-INCH DICE

TWO 8-OUNCE BOTTLES CLAM JUICE
  OR 2 CUPS REDUCED-SODIUM
  CHICKEN BROTH
1 CUP HALF-AND-HALF OR MILK
2 TO 2½ POUNDS COD, HADDOCK, OR
  OCEAN PERCH FILLETS, CUT INTO
  1½-INCH PIECES

1. In a large saucepan, cook the bacon over medium heat until it is browned and crisp, about 10 minutes. Transfer the bacon to paper towels to drain and set aside. Pour off all but 2 tablespoons of the fat.

2. In the same saucepan, warm the butter in the bacon fat until the butter is melted. Add the onions, salt, pepper, and thyme, and sauté until the onions are tender and lightly golden but not browned, about 5 minutes.

3. Add the potato and stir well to coat. Stir in the clam juice and half-and-half, and bring to a boil. Reduce the heat to low, cover the pan, and simmer until the potato is just tender, 5 to 7 minutes.

4. Add the fish and reserved bacon, cover, and simmer gently until the fish is firm and just opaque, 5 to 10 minutes.

5. Ladle the chowder into 4 soup bowls and serve hot.

SWEET AFTERTHOUGHT: *Using a fudgy-style brownie mix, pour ½ inch of batter into a muffin tin lined with paper muffin cups; watch them carefully, as the cooking time for these mini-brownies will be much shorter than for a full pan. When the brownies are cool, fill the muffin cups (still in the muffin tin) with softened ice cream and place in the freezer to firm up. Serve the ice cream-topped brownies with chocolate sauce.*

TOMATO-CLAM
CHOWDER WITH GARLIC TOASTS

SERVES 6

◆ EXTRA-QUICK ◇ LOW-FAT

ONE 16-OUNCE CAN NO-SALT-ADDED
   WHOLE TOMATOES
1 CUP CHICKEN BROTH, PREFERABLY
   REDUCED-SODIUM
2 GARLIC CLOVES, MINCED
½ TEASPOON SUGAR
¼ TEASPOON BLACK PEPPER
2 MEDIUM ALL-PURPOSE POTATOES,
   PEELED AND CUBED

2 TABLESPOONS OLIVE OIL
½ CUP BOTTLED CLAM JUICE OR
   CHICKEN BROTH
2 TEASPOONS CORNSTARCH
8 SLICES (½-INCH-THICK) FRENCH OR
   ITALIAN BREAD
4 SCALLIONS, COARSELY CHOPPED
ONE 6½-OUNCE CAN MINCED CLAMS,
   DRAINED

1. In a medium saucepan, combine the tomatoes, broth, half of the garlic, the sugar, and pepper, and break up the tomatoes with the back of a spoon. Cover and bring the mixture to a boil over medium-high heat. Add the potatoes, reduce the heat to medium-low, cover, and simmer until the potatoes are tender, about 15 minutes.

2. Meanwhile, in a small skillet, warm the oil over medium heat. Add the remaining garlic and cook, stirring constantly, until the garlic is fragrant, 1 to 2 minutes. Remove the pan from the heat and set aside. In a small bowl, blend the clam juice with the cornstarch.

3. Preheat the oven to 400°. Line a baking sheet with foil.

4. Brush both sides of the bread with the garlic oil and place them on the prepared baking sheet. Bake for 8 minutes, or until golden.

5. Return the broth mixture to a boil over medium-high heat. Stir the clam juice mixture to reblend, add it to the boiling broth, and cook, stirring constantly, until the liquid is slightly thickened, about 1 minute.

6. Stir in the scallions and clams. Reduce the heat to medium-low and simmer just until the clams are heated through, about 2 minutes. Serve the chowder hot with the garlic crostini on the side.

Boston Crab Chowder with Nutmeg Croutons

SERVES 4

- 4 TABLESPOONS UNSALTED BUTTER
- 2 GARLIC CLOVES, MINCED
- 5 SCALLIONS, COARSELY CHOPPED
- 3 TABLESPOONS FLOUR
- 2 CUPS REDUCED-SODIUM CHICKEN BROTH
- 1 MEDIUM ALL-PURPOSE POTATO, PEELED AND CUT INTO ½-INCH CUBES
- 2 MEDIUM CARROTS, COARSELY CHOPPED
- ¾ TEASPOON NUTMEG
- ¼ TEASPOON PEPPER, PREFERABLY WHITE
- 2 SLICES FIRM-TEXTURED WHITE BREAD, TOASTED
- ONE 6-OUNCE CAN CRABMEAT, DRAINED
- 1 CELERY RIB, COARSELY CHOPPED
- 2 CUPS LOW-FAT MILK

1. In a large saucepan, warm 3 tablespoons of the butter over medium-high heat until melted. Add the garlic and scallions, and cook, stirring, until the scallions are wilted, about 2 minutes.

2. Stir in the flour and cook, stirring, until the flour is no longer visible, about 30 seconds. Gradually pour in the broth, stirring constantly to keep the mixture smooth. Bring to a boil, then add the potato, carrots, ¼ teaspoon of the nutmeg, and the pepper. Let the mixture return to a boil, then reduce the heat to medium-low, cover, and simmer until the potato is tender, about 15 minutes.

3. Meanwhile, in a small saucepan, combine the remaining 1 tablespoon butter with the remaining ½ teaspoon nutmeg, and cook over low heat until fragrant, about 1 minute. Brush the toast with the nutmeg butter and cut into small triangles.

4. Increase the heat under the broth mixture to medium and bring it to a simmer. Add the crabmeat, celery, and milk, and cook, stirring, until heated through, 3 to 4 minutes. Serve the chowder with the nutmeg croutons.

Italian-Style Fish Fillets

SERVES 4

◇ LOW-FAT

1½ TABLESPOONS OLIVE OIL

8 SCALLIONS, COARSELY CHOPPED

3 GARLIC CLOVES, MINCED

1 CUP CANNED CRUSHED TOMATOES

1 TABLESPOON TOMATO PASTE

1 TEASPOON BASIL

¼ TEASPOON BLACK PEPPER

1 LARGE YELLOW SQUASH, CUT INTO
THIN ROUNDS

1½ POUNDS HADDOCK OR SEA BASS
FILLETS, CUT INTO 1-INCH PIECES

¼ CUP CHOPPED PARSLEY (OPTIONAL)

1. In a large skillet, warm the oil over medium-high heat. Add the scallions and garlic, and cook, stirring frequently, until the garlic begins to brown, about 5 minutes.

2. Add the crushed tomatoes, tomato paste, basil, and pepper, and bring to a boil. Reduce the heat to medium-low, cover, and simmer for 10 minutes. Add the squash, cover, and simmer until the squash is crisp-tender, about 5 minutes.

3. Add the fish to the simmering sauce, increase the heat slightly, cover, and cook until the fish is still firm but just flakes when tested with a fork, about 10 minutes.

4. Stir in the parsley (if using) and serve hot.

Substitution: *Other types of summer squash, such as zucchini or pattypan, can be used instead of the yellow squash. If you can find it, try golden zucchini, which has a delicate flavor reminiscent of sweet corn.*

Fish Curry with Spinach and Peanuts

SERVES 4

♦ EXTRA-QUICK

1 TABLESPOON OLIVE OIL

1 TABLESPOON UNSALTED BUTTER

3 GARLIC CLOVES, MINCED

1 MEDIUM ONION, COARSELY CHOPPED

3 TABLESPOONS FLOUR

2 TABLESPOONS CURRY POWDER

1 CUP CHICKEN BROTH, PREFERABLY
REDUCED-SODIUM

¼ TEASPOON BLACK PEPPER

PINCH OF CAYENNE PEPPER

½ CUP (PACKED) CILANTRO SPRIGS,
MINCED

1 POUND COD OR HADDOCK FILLETS,
CUT INTO 1-INCH PIECES

ONE 10-OUNCE PACKAGE FROZEN
CHOPPED SPINACH, THAWED AND
SQUEEZED DRY

¼ CUP REDUCED-FAT SOUR CREAM

⅓ CUP UNSALTED DRY-ROASTED
PEANUTS

1. In a large skillet, warm the oil with the butter over medium-high heat until the butter is melted. Add the garlic and onion, and cook, stirring, until the onion is just translucent, about 3 minutes.

2. Stir in the flour and curry powder, and cook, stirring, until the flour is no longer visible, about 30 seconds. Stir in the broth, black pepper, cayenne and 2 tablespoons of the cilantro. Bring the mixture to a boil, stirring constantly.

3. Add the fish and spinach to the boiling curry mixture. Reduce the heat to low, cover, and simmer until the fish just flakes when tested with a fork, about 5 minutes.

4. Remove the fish curry from the heat and gently stir in the sour cream, peanuts, and remaining cilantro. Serve hot.

SPICY FISH RAGOUT OVER LEMON RICE

SERVES 4

1 CUP RICE

2 TABLESPOONS FRESH LEMON JUICE

1 TABLESPOON UNSALTED BUTTER

2 TEASPOONS GRATED LEMON ZEST

⅜ TEASPOON CAYENNE PEPPER

2 TABLESPOONS OLIVE OIL

2 MEDIUM ONIONS, COARSELY CHOPPED

3 GARLIC CLOVES, MINCED

¼ POUND MUSHROOMS, THINLY SLICED

3 MEDIUM PLUM TOMATOES, COARSELY CHOPPED

1 LARGE GREEN BELL PEPPER, CUT INTO 1-INCH SQUARES

½ CUP BOTTLED CLAM JUICE OR CHICKEN BROTH

½ CUP DRY WHITE WINE OR CHICKEN BROTH

4 TABLESPOONS TOMATO PASTE

½ TEASPOON SALT

½ TEASPOON BLACK PEPPER

¼ TEASPOON RED PEPPER FLAKES

1 POUND RED SNAPPER OR SEA BASS FILLETS, CUT INTO 1-INCH CHUNKS

1. In a medium saucepan, bring 2 cups of water to a boil over high heat. Add the rice, lemon juice, butter, lemon zest, and ¼ teaspoon of the cayenne. Reduce the heat to low, cover, and simmer until the rice is tender and all the liquid is absorbed, about 20 minutes.

2. Meanwhile, in a large skillet, warm the oil over medium-high heat. Add the onions and garlic, and stir-fry until the onions begin to brown, about 5 minutes.

3. Stir in the mushrooms, tomatoes, bell pepper, clam juice, wine, tomato paste, salt, black pepper, red pepper flakes, and the remaining ⅛ teaspoon cayenne. Bring the mixture to a boil and add the fish. Reduce the heat to low, cover, and simmer until the fish just flakes when tested with a fork, about 7 minutes.

4. Uncover the skillet, increase the heat to medium-high, and cook until the liquid is slightly reduced, 1 to 2 minutes. Serve the ragout over the rice.

CURRIED FLOUNDER WITH MUSHROOMS

SERVES 4

◇ LOW-FAT

1 TABLESPOON CHOPPED FRESH GINGER
½ TEASPOON TURMERIC
¼ TEASPOON CUMIN
¼ TEASPOON GROUND CORIANDER
⅛ TEASPOON FENNEL SEEDS
⅛ TEASPOON NUTMEG
1 TABLESPOON OLIVE OIL
2 LARGE ONIONS, SLICED
ONE 14½-OUNCE CAN NO-SALT-ADDED
   WHOLE TOMATOES, DRAINED AND
   CHOPPED

2 CUPS FISH BROTH, BOTTLED CLAM
   JUICE, OR REDUCED-SODIUM
   CHICKEN BROTH
1 POUND MUSHROOMS, HALVED
1 TABLESPOON FRESH LEMON JUICE
1 POUND FLOUNDER OR SOLE FILLETS,
   CUT INTO 1-INCH-WIDE STRIPS

1. With a mortar and pestle (or in a mini-food processor), grind together the ginger, turmeric, cumin, coriander, fennel seeds, and nutmeg to form a paste. Set the paste aside.

2. In a large skillet, warm the oil over medium-high heat. Add the onions and cook, stirring frequently, until they are translucent, about 4 minutes.

3. Stir in the spice paste, tomatoes, and broth, and bring the liquid to a boil. Add the mushrooms and lemon juice. Reduce the heat to low and simmer the curry until it is reduced by half, 10 to 12 minutes.

4. Lay the fish strips on top of the curry, cover the skillet, and steam the fish until it is opaque, about 2 minutes. Serve hot.

CARIBBEAN RED SNAPPER STEW

SERVES 4

◇ LOW-FAT

¼ CUP DRY WHITE WINE

2 TABLESPOONS DARK RUM

1 TABLESPOON MINCED FRESH GINGER

1 GARLIC CLOVE, MINCED

¼ TEASPOON BLACK PEPPER

1 POUND RED SNAPPER OR SEA BASS
   FILLETS, CUT INTO 1½-INCH
   SQUARES

1 TABLESPOON OLIVE OIL

1 MEDIUM ONION, CUT INTO SMALL
   CHUNKS

2 TABLESPOONS FLOUR

2 TEASPOONS TOMATO PASTE

1 MEDIUM GREEN BELL PEPPER, CUT
   INTO ¾-INCH PIECES

2 CUPS FISH BROTH, BOTTLED CLAM
   JUICE, OR REDUCED-SODIUM
   CHICKEN BROTH

2 MEDIUM TOMATOES, COARSELY
   CHOPPED

1 MEDIUM MANGO, PEELED AND CUT
   INTO ¾-INCH PIECES

¼ TEASPOON SALT

1. In a bowl, combine the wine, rum, ginger, garlic, and black pepper. Marinate the fish pieces in this mixture for 30 minutes in the refrigerator.

2. In a large pot, warm the oil over medium heat. Add the onion and cook, stirring occasionally, until it begins to brown, 6 to 8 minutes. Stir in the flour, then the tomato paste and bell pepper. Gradually whisk in the broth.

Drain the marinade from the fish and add it to the pot. Bring the liquid to a simmer and cook for 3 minutes.

3. Add the fish, tomatoes, mango, and salt. Cover the pot, reduce the heat to medium-low, and simmer the stew until the fish is opaque and flakes easily, about 7 minutes. Serve hot.

SEAFOOD STEW
with WATER CHESTNUTS

SERVES 4

◇ LOW - FAT

¼ CUP SHERRY

2 TABLESPOONS MINCED FRESH GINGER

1 GARLIC CLOVE, MINCED

¼ TEASPOON BLACK PEPPER

¾ POUND RED SNAPPER OR GROUPER
    FILLETS, CUT INTO 1-INCH CUBES

½ POUND LARGE SHRIMP, SHELLED AND
    DEVEINED

1 TABLESPOON VEGETABLE OIL

1 CUP BOTTLED CLAM JUICE OR
    REDUCED-SODIUM CHICKEN BROTH

1 TEASPOON SOY SAUCE

2 MEDIUM CARROTS, THINLY SLICED
    DIAGONALLY

4 SCALLIONS, THINLY SLICED
    DIAGONALLY

8 CANNED WATER CHESTNUTS, THINLY
    SLICED

¼ POUND MUSHROOMS, THINLY SLICED

4 TEASPOONS CORNSTARCH BLENDED
    WITH 2 TABLESPOONS WATER

1 BUNCH OF WATERCRESS, STEMMED

1. In a medium bowl, combine the sherry, ginger, garlic, and pepper, and mix well. Add the fish and shrimp, stir to coat with the marinade, and let the mixture marinate at room temperature for 20 minutes.

2. Drain and reserve the marinade. In a Dutch oven, warm the oil over medium-high heat. Add the fish and shrimp, and stir-fry until they are opaque, 2 to 3 minutes. Transfer the seafood to a plate and set aside.

3. Add the clam juice, soy sauce, and reserved marinade to the Dutch oven, and stir

to blend. Add the carrots, scallions, water chestnuts, and mushrooms. Bring the mixture to a boil over high heat, reduce the heat to low, cover, and simmer until the carrots are tender, about 8 minutes.

4. Stir the cornstarch mixture into the simmering carrot mixture along with the watercress and reserved seafood. Return the stew to a boil and cook, stirring constantly, until the stew is slightly thickened, about 2 minutes.

COD STEWED WITH POTATOES, CORN, AND TOMATOES

SERVES 6

◇ LOW-FAT

1 TABLESPOON OLIVE OIL

1 POUND ONIONS, THINLY SLICED

2 POUNDS UNPEELED SMALL RED
  POTATOES, THINLY SLICED

2 CUPS FRESH OR FROZEN CORN
  KERNELS, THAWED

½ CUP DICED GREEN BELL PEPPER

HOT PEPPER SAUCE

1 POUND COD FILLETS, CUT INTO
  CHUNKS

ONE 28-OUNCE CAN NO-SALT-ADDED
  WHOLE TOMATOES, DRAINED AND
  CHOPPED

½ TEASPOON SALT

½ TEASPOON BLACK PEPPER

1. In a large pot, warm the oil over medium heat. Add a layer of onions and a layer of potatoes. Sprinkle some of the corn and bell pepper on top. Dribble a few drops of the hot pepper sauce over the vegetables. Add a layer of fish and tomatoes, and season with a pinch each of the salt and black pepper.

2. Repeat the process, building up successive layers, until the remaining vegetables and fish are used. Cover the pot, reduce the heat to medium-low, and cook until the potatoes are tender, about 45 minutes.

3. Serve the stew hot.

SWEET AFTERTHOUGHT: *Purée a 10-ounce package of frozen raspberries in syrup (break the frozen berries into large chunks, then process them in a food processor). Toast slices of pound cake under the broiler or in a toaster oven, then top them with scoops of ice cream and drizzle with the raspberry syrup. Serve immediately.*

Quick Cioppino
with Parsley Toasts

SERVES 4 TO 6

1 TABLESPOON OLIVE OIL

1 LARGE ONION, COARSELY CHOPPED

5 GARLIC CLOVES, MINCED

3 TABLESPOONS UNSALTED BUTTER

1 LARGE GREEN BELL PEPPER, COARSELY CHOPPED

½ POUND MUSHROOMS, COARSELY CHOPPED

6 CANNED NO-SALT-ADDED WHOLE TOMATOES, DRAINED AND CHOPPED

2 CUPS REDUCED-SODIUM CHICKEN BROTH

⅔ CUP DRY RED WINE

2 TABLESPOONS TOMATO PASTE

PINCH OF SUGAR

¾ TEASPOON BLACK PEPPER

4 PARSLEY SPRIGS, MINCED

1 MEDIUM LOAF OF ITALIAN BREAD, HALVED LENGTHWISE

½ POUND STRIPED BASS OR RED SNAPPER FILLETS, CUT INTO 1-INCH CHUNKS

ONE 6-OUNCE CAN CRABMEAT

1. In a large skillet, warm 2 teaspoons of the oil over medium-high heat. Add the onion and garlic, and stir-fry until the onion begins to brown, about 5 minutes.

2. Add the remaining 1 teaspoon oil, 1 tablespoon of the butter, the bell pepper and mushrooms, and cook, stirring, until the pepper begins to soften, about 3 minutes.

3. Add the tomatoes, broth, wine, tomato paste, sugar, and ½ teaspoon of the black pepper. Bring the mixture to a boil, then reduce the heat to low, cover, and simmer while you prepare the remaining ingredients.

4. Preheat the broiler or a toaster oven. In a small bowl, blend the remaining 2 tablespoons butter with the parsley and remaining ¼ teaspoon black pepper. Spread the cut sides of the bread with the parsley butter. Broil the bread until lightly toasted, then cut into 4-inch lengths.

5. Uncover the tomato mixture and return it to a boil over medium-high heat. Add the fish and cook until it just flakes when tested with a fork, about 6 minutes.

6. Stir in the crabmeat and cook until just heated through, about 3 minutes. Serve with the parsley toasts on the side.

BLACKENED SEAFOOD STEW

SERVES 4 TO 6

2 TABLESPOONS UNSALTED BUTTER

1 CELERY RIB, THINLY SLICED

1 MEDIUM ONION, COARSELY CHOPPED

1 MEDIUM GREEN BELL PEPPER,
   COARSELY CHOPPED

2 TABLESPOONS VEGETABLE OIL

2 POUNDS RED SNAPPER OR OCEAN
   PERCH FILLETS

½ TEASPOON CAYENNE PEPPER

½ TEASPOON SALT

½ TEASPOON BLACK PEPPER

16 MEDIUM SHRIMP, SHELLED AND
   DEVEINED

2½ CUPS FISH BROTH, BOTTLED CLAM
   JUICE, OR REDUCED-SODIUM
   CHICKEN BROTH

2 MEDIUM TOMATOES, CUT INTO
   8 WEDGES

ONE 10-OUNCE PACKAGE FROZEN
   CORN KERNELS, THAWED

2 TABLESPOONS MINCED FRESH DILL,
   OR 2 TEASPOONS DRIED

1. In a Dutch oven, warm the butter over medium-high heat. Add the celery, onion, and bell pepper, and cook, stirring frequently, until tender, 10 to 12 minutes.

2. Meanwhile, in a large cast-iron skillet, warm the oil over high heat until smoking. Sprinkle the fish fillets on both sides with the cayenne, salt, and black pepper. Add the fish fillets and sear until they are dark golden brown, about 2 minutes per side. Transfer the fish to a plate.

3. Add the shrimp to the skillet and sear for 1 minute on each side. Transfer the shrimp to a separate plate.

4. Add the broth, tomatoes, and corn to the vegetables in the Dutch oven. Bring to a boil, then reduce the heat to medium-low and simmer for 5 minutes.

5. Meanwhile, cut the seared fish fillets into 2-inch pieces and add to the Dutch oven along with the dill. Add the shrimp, return the stew to a simmer, and cook until the fish is firm and opaque and the shrimp are pink, 4 to 5 minutes. Serve hot.

New Orleans Fish and Oyster Stew

SERVES 4 TO 6

4 TABLESPOONS UNSALTED BUTTER

1 MEDIUM RED BELL PEPPER, FINELY CHOPPED

1 MEDIUM GREEN BELL PEPPER, FINELY CHOPPED

¾ CUP FINELY CHOPPED SHALLOTS OR ONION

2 CELERY RIBS, FINELY CHOPPED

2 GARLIC CLOVES, MINCED

1½ TEASPOONS CHOPPED FRESH OREGANO, OR ½ TEASPOON DRIED

1½ CUPS HALF-AND-HALF

1 CUP FISH BROTH, BOTTLED CLAM JUICE, OR REDUCED-SODIUM CHICKEN BROTH

1 FRESH JALAPEÑO PEPPER, SEEDED AND MINCED (OPTIONAL)

¾ TEASPOON PAPRIKA

½ TEASPOON CURRY POWDER

½ TEASPOON SALT

¼ TEASPOON CUMIN

¼ TEASPOON WHITE PEPPER

PINCH OF CAYENNE PEPPER

2 POUNDS HALIBUT, SWORDFISH, OR COD FILLETS, CUT INTO 1-INCH PIECES

12 TO 16 SHUCKED OYSTERS, WITH THEIR JUICES

1. In a large skillet, warm the butter over medium heat until melted. Add the bell peppers, shallots, and celery, and sauté, stirring frequently, until tender, 8 to 10 minutes.

2. Add the garlic and oregano, and cook for 30 seconds. Add the half-and-half and broth, increase the heat to medium-high, and bring to a boil. Stir in the jalapeño (if using), paprika, curry powder, salt, cumin, white pepper, and cayenne pepper.

3. Add the fish to the skillet, reduce the heat to medium-low, and simmer just until the fish is firm and turns opaque, 4 to 5 minutes.

4. Add the oysters and their juices, and simmer just until the edges of the oysters start to curl, about 30 seconds.

RAGOUT OF SCALLOPS AND RED PEPPERS

SERVES 4

2 MEDIUM RED BELL PEPPERS, CUT
   INTO 3 OR 4 FLAT PANELS, CORES
   AND SEEDS DISCARDED
1 POUND SEA SCALLOPS, HALVED IF
   LARGE
¼ TEASPOON BLACK PEPPER
1 TABLESPOON FRESH LIME JUICE
2 TABLESPOONS RED WINE VINEGAR
2 TEASPOONS FRESH THYME, OR
   ½ TEASPOON DRIED

2 TABLESPOONS OLIVE OIL
½ POUND MUSHROOMS, QUARTERED
¼ TEASPOON SALT
½ CUP DRY WHITE WINE
1 BUNCH SCALLIONS, CUT INTO
   1-INCH PIECES
2 BELGIAN ENDIVES, CUT CROSSWISE
   INTO 1-INCH PIECES

1. Preheat the broiler. Place the pepper pieces, skin-side up, on a baking sheet and broil as close to the heat as possible for 10 minutes, or until evenly charred.

2. Meanwhile, place the scallops in a bowl and sprinkle them with ⅛ teaspoon of the black pepper and the lime juice. Set aside.

3. Transfer the broiled peppers to a bowl, cover with a plate, and let steam for 1 to 2 minutes. Working over the bowl to catch their juices, peel the peppers. In a food processor or blender, combine the roasted peppers with their reserved juices, the vinegar, thyme, and remaining ⅛ teaspoon black pepper; purée the mixture until it is smooth.

4. In a large skillet, warm the oil over medium-high heat. Add the mushrooms and sauté, stirring frequently, for 3 minutes. Sprinkle the mushrooms with ⅛ teaspoon of the salt, then pour in the wine. Cook the mixture, stirring occasionally, until almost all the liquid has evaporated, 3 to 5 minutes.

5. Pour the red pepper purée into the skillet. Place the scallops on top, sprinkle them with the remaining ⅛ teaspoon of salt, and cook the mixture for 1 minute, stirring frequently. Add the scallions and endives, and cook, stirring frequently, until the scallops are firm and just opaque, 2 to 3 minutes. Serve hot.

CREOLE-STYLE SCALLOPS AND RICE

SERVES 4

◇ LOW-FAT

1 TABLESPOON OLIVE OIL

3 GARLIC CLOVES, MINCED

1 LARGE ONION, COARSELY CHOPPED

1¾ CUPS TOMATO-VEGETABLE JUICE

2 CELERY RIBS, COARSELY CHOPPED

1 LARGE GREEN BELL PEPPER, CUT INTO
   THIN STRIPS

¼ CUP (PACKED) PARSLEY SPRIGS,
   COARSELY CHOPPED

1 TABLESPOON FRESH LIME JUICE

1 TABLESPOON TOMATO PASTE

1 TEASPOON GRATED LIME ZEST

4 DROPS OF HOT PEPPER SAUCE

1½ TEASPOONS BASIL

½ TEASPOON BLACK PEPPER

PINCH OF CAYENNE PEPPER

1 CUP RICE

¾ POUND SEA SCALLOPS, QUARTERED

1. In a large nonstick skillet, warm the oil over medium-high heat. Add the garlic and onion, and stir-fry until the onion just begins to brown, about 4 minutes.

2. Stir in the tomato-vegetable juice, celery, bell pepper, 2 tablespoons of the parsley, the lime juice, tomato paste, lime zest, hot pepper sauce, basil, black pepper, and cayenne. Add the rice and bring to a boil. Reduce the heat to low, cover, and simmer until the rice is not quite tender, 15 to 20 minutes.

3. Stir in the scallops and the remaining 2 tablespoons parsley. Cover and simmer until the scallops are just cooked through, 3 to 5 minutes. Serve hot.

Variation: *For a dinner party version of this dish, use lobster in place of some or all of the scallops. Cut lobster tail meat into chunks approximately the same size as the scallops. You could also use ½ cup of dry white wine to replace some of the tomato-vegetable juice. Add the wine at the end of Step 1 to infuse the onion with flavor.*

Mexican-Style Shrimp with Pasta and Tomatoes

SERVES 4

3 TABLESPOONS VEGETABLE OIL

½ POUND VERMICELLI, BROKEN INTO
2-INCH-LONG PIECES

1 MEDIUM ONION, CHOPPED

1½ CUPS CHOPPED TOMATOES

ONE 4-OUNCE CAN CHOPPED MILD
GREEN CHILIES, DRAINED

1 GARLIC CLOVE, LIGHTLY CRUSHED
AND PEELED

2 CUPS REDUCED-SODIUM CHICKEN
BROTH

¼ TEASPOON SALT

¼ TEASPOON BLACK PEPPER

1 POUND MEDIUM SHRIMP, SHELLED
AND DEVEINED

1 TABLESPOON CHOPPED CILANTRO

1 CUP REDUCED-FAT SOUR CREAM

1. In a large skillet, warm the oil over medium-high heat. Add the vermicelli and sauté, stirring constantly to prevent burning, until golden, 1 to 2 minutes.

2. Drain off any excess oil from the pan. Add the onion, tomatoes, green chilies, and garlic to the vermicelli, and stir well to combine.

3. Add the broth, salt, and pepper, and bring the mixture to a boil. Reduce the heat to low, cover, and simmer for 15 minutes.

4. Add the shrimp and stir to combine. Cover and cook until the shrimp begin to curl and are pink, 2 to 3 minutes.

5. Sprinkle the shrimp and tomato mixture with the cilantro. Serve with the sour cream on the side.

KITCHEN NOTE: *Shelling and deveining shrimp is one of the most time-consuming preparation chores. Although many fish stores sell already-shelled shrimp, they also charge an exorbitant price for the convenience. Consider instead purchasing a shrimp sheller/deveiner. These relatively inexpensive gadgets come in a variety of forms, but they all make short work of this tedious kitchen task.*

SHRIMP CURRY WITH COCONUT-ALMOND RICE

SERVES 4

2¾ CUPS CHICKEN BROTH, PREFERABLY
   REDUCED-SODIUM
1 CUP RICE
2 TABLESPOONS OLIVE OIL
3 GARLIC CLOVES, MINCED
1 MEDIUM ONION, COARSELY CHOPPED
1 POUND MEDIUM SHRIMP, SHELLED
   AND DEVEINED
1 LARGE GREEN BELL PEPPER, CUT INTO
   1-INCH PIECES

3 TABLESPOONS CURRY POWDER
1 TABLESPOON FLOUR
½ CUP LOW-FAT MILK
¼ CUP (PACKED) CILANTRO SPRIGS
   (OPTIONAL)
⅓ CUP SWEETENED SHREDDED
   COCONUT
¼ CUP SLICED ALMONDS

1. In a medium saucepan, bring 2 cups of the broth to a boil over high heat. Add the rice, reduce the heat to low, cover, and cook until the rice is tender, about 20 minutes.

2. Meanwhile, in a large skillet, warm 1 tablespoon of the oil over medium-high heat. Add the garlic and onion, and stir-fry until the onion begins to brown, about 3 minutes.

3. Stir in the remaining 1 tablespoon oil, the shrimp, and bell pepper, and stir-fry for 2 minutes. Stir in the curry powder and flour, and cook, stirring, until the flour and curry powder are completely incorporated.

4. Stir in the remaining ¾ cup broth, the milk, and cilantro (if using), and bring to a boil. Reduce the heat to medium-low, cover, and simmer until the shrimp are cooked through and the bell pepper is tender, about 2 minutes.

5. When the rice is done, stir in the coconut and almonds. Serve the rice with the shrimp curry spooned on top.

Shrimp with Green Chili Creole Sauce

SERVES 4

1 TABLESPOON OLIVE OIL

1 TABLESPOON UNSALTED BUTTER

1 MEDIUM ONION, COARSELY CHOPPED

3 GARLIC CLOVES, MINCED

ONE 16-OUNCE CAN NO-SALT-ADDED
WHOLE TOMATOES

TWO 4-OUNCE CANS CHOPPED MILD
GREEN CHILIES, DRAINED

½ TEASPOON DRY MUSTARD

¼ TEASPOON BLACK PEPPER

¼ TEASPOON RED PEPPER FLAKES

PINCH OF SUGAR

1 TABLESPOON CORNSTARCH

¼ CUP CHICKEN BROTH

1 POUND MEDIUM SHRIMP, SHELLED
AND DEVEINED

1 LARGE YELLOW OR GREEN BELL
PEPPER, CUT INTO BITE-SIZE PIECES

¼ CUP CHOPPED PARSLEY (OPTIONAL)

1. In a large skillet, warm the oil with the butter over medium-high heat until the butter is melted. Add the onion and garlic, and stir-fry until the mixture begins to brown, about 5 minutes.

2. Add the tomatoes, green chilies, mustard, black pepper, red pepper flakes, and sugar, and bring to a boil, breaking up the tomatoes with the back of a spoon. Reduce the heat to low, cover, and simmer for 10 minutes.

3. Meanwhile, in a small bowl, combine the cornstarch and broth, stir to blend, and set aside.

4. Uncover the tomato sauce and return it to a boil over medium-high heat. Add the shrimp, bell pepper, cornstarch mixture, and parsley (if using). Cook, stirring constantly, until the shrimp are cooked through, the bell pepper is tender, and the sauce has thickened slightly, 3 to 4 minutes.

ORIENTAL OVEN-STEAMED FISH WITH VEGETABLES

SERVES 4

◇ LOW-FAT

3 TABLESPOONS REDUCED-SODIUM SOY
   SAUCE
1 TABLESPOON ORIENTAL (DARK)
   SESAME OIL
2 GARLIC CLOVES, MINCED
¼ TEASPOON RED PEPPER FLAKES
¼ TEASPOON BLACK PEPPER
1 LARGE CARROT, CUT INTO VERY THIN
   MATCHSTICKS

4 SCALLIONS, COARSELY CHOPPED
½-INCH PIECE OF FRESH GINGER, CUT
   INTO THIN SLIVERS
1½ POUNDS COD, RED SNAPPER, OR
   SEA BASS FILLETS
¼ POUND SNOW PEAS
¼ CUP CHOPPED CILANTRO
   (OPTIONAL)

1. Preheat the oven to 400°. Line a shallow baking pan large enough to hold the fish in one layer with foil.

2. In a small bowl, combine the soy sauce, sesame oil, garlic, red pepper flakes, and black pepper.

3. Scatter half the carrot, scallions, and ginger over the bottom of the prepared baking pan. Place the fish fillets, in one layer, on top.

4. Scatter the snow peas and the remaining carrot, scallions, and ginger on top of the fish. Drizzle the soy sauce mixture evenly over everything.

5. Cover tightly with foil and bake until the fish is opaque throughout and just flakes when tested with a fork, 15 to 20 minutes.

6. Serve the fish with some of the vegetables, and a sprinkling of cilantro, if desired.

STEAMED FISH WITH GINGER, SCALLIONS, AND CILANTRO

SERVES 4

◆ EXTRA - QUICK

1½ POUNDS HALIBUT, SEA BASS, OR
    RED SNAPPER FILLETS
½ TEASPOON SALT
½ TEASPOON BLACK PEPPER
1 TABLESPOON MINCED SCALLIONS

1 TABLESPOON MINCED CILANTRO
1 TEASPOON MINCED FRESH GINGER
1½ TABLESPOONS OLIVE OIL

1. Bring 1 inch of water to a boil in a small covered roasting pan.

2. Place the fish on a heatproof platter and set on a rack or metal trivet. Sprinkle the fish with the salt and pepper, and scatter the scallions, cilantro, and ginger over them.

3. Place the rack and platter in the roasting pan. Cover the roasting pan tightly with foil and steam the fish for 8 to 12 minutes, depending on their thickness, or until they just flake when tested with a fork.

4. Just before serving, in small saucepan, warm the olive oil over low heat. Drizzle the oil over the steamed fish.

VARIATION: *To give this dish the robust flavors of Provence, use grated orange zest in place of the cilantro, and garlic in place of the ginger. If you have Pernod (or other anise-flavored liquor, such as Ricard) on hand, add a splash to the fish before steaming. If possible, use an extra-virgin olive oil, which is more deeply flavored than virgin or light olive oils.*

Chinese-Style Poached Fish Fillets

SERVES 4

2 SCALLIONS, SPLIT LENGTHWISE

FOUR QUARTER-SIZE SLICES FRESH
GINGER, PLUS 1 TABLESPOON
MINCED

3 TABLESPOONS DRY SHERRY

¾ CUP CHICKEN BROTH

¼ CUP RED WINE VINEGAR

3 TABLESPOONS REDUCED-SODIUM SOY
SAUCE

3 TABLESPOONS SUGAR

4 LARGE FLOUNDER OR SOLE FILLETS
(ABOUT 2 POUNDS TOTAL)

2 TABLESPOONS VEGETABLE OIL

2 GARLIC CLOVES, LIGHTLY CRUSHED
AND PEELED

4 TEASPOONS CORNSTARCH BLENDED
WITH 2 TABLESPOONS WATER

1 TABLESPOON ORIENTAL (DARK)
SESAME OIL

1. In a Dutch oven, bring 2 inches of water to a boil. Add the scallions, sliced ginger, and 2 tablespoons of the sherry.

2. Meanwhile, in a small bowl, combine the chicken broth, vinegar, soy sauce, sugar, and remaining 1 tablespoon sherry.

3. Add the fish to the boiling water, cover, and remove from the heat. The fish should be done in 1 to 1½ minutes, depending on their thickness. Gently lift the fillets out, one at a time, with a wide slotted spatula. Drain well and arrange on a serving platter; cover loosely with foil to keep warm.

4. In a small saucepan, warm the vegetable oil over medium heat. Add the garlic and minced ginger, and stir-fry until fragrant, about 30 seconds. Discard the garlic. Add the sherry-soy sauce mixture and bring to a boil over high heat.

5. Stir the cornstarch mixture thoroughly and slowly add it to the sauce, stirring constantly to prevent lumping. Bring to a boil and simmer for 30 seconds. Remove from the heat and stir in the sesame oil.

6. Pour the sauce over the fish and serve hot.

35

FILLETS OF FLOUNDER CAPRI

SERVES 4

4 FLOUNDER OR SOLE FILLETS (ABOUT
  1½ POUNDS TOTAL)
3 TABLESPOONS UNSALTED BUTTER
⅓ CUP BOTTLED CLAM JUICE OR
  CHICKEN BROTH
⅓ CUP DRY WHITE WINE OR DRY
  VERMOUTH

¼ TEASPOON MINCED GARLIC
1 TEASPOON DIJON MUSTARD
1 SMALL BAY LEAF
1 TABLESPOON CHOPPED PARSLEY
1 LARGE TOMATO, COARSELY CHOPPED
½ TEASPOON WHITE PEPPER
½ CUP HEAVY CREAM

1. Cut the fillets in half lengthwise and roll each half, starting with the widest portion, into a plump little jelly roll. Preheat the oven to 200°.

2. Coat the bottom of a large skillet with 2 tablespoons of the butter. Add the clam juice, wine, garlic, mustard, bay leaf, parsley, tomato, and pepper. Bring to a boil. Standing the fish rolls on end, arrange them in the skillet and simmer for 6 minutes, basting once or twice.

3. With a slotted spoon, transfer the fish rolls to a heatproof serving platter and keep warm in the oven.

4. Add the cream to the skillet and gently simmer over medium heat, stirring constantly, until the sauce thickens and coats the back of a spoon, about 3 minutes. Remove the skillet from the heat and swirl in the remaining 1 tablespoon butter. Pour the sauce over the fish.

COD BASQUE-STYLE

SERVES 4

¼ CUP OLIVE OIL

1 SMALL ONION, COARSELY CHOPPED

1 MEDIUM ALL-PURPOSE POTATO,
PEELED AND CUT INTO PAPER-THIN
SLICES

4 COD FILLETS (½ TO 1 INCH THICK,
ABOUT 2 POUNDS TOTAL)

1½ CUPS BOTTLED CLAM JUICE OR
REDUCED-SODIUM CHICKEN BROTH

1 GARLIC CLOVE, MINCED

⅓ CUP CHOPPED PARSLEY

½ TEASPOON BLACK PEPPER

1. In a large skillet, warm the oil over medium heat. Add the onion and cook, stirring, until softened but not browned, about 1 minute. Reduce the heat to low, add the potato slices, and cook, covered, until the potatoes soften and begin to fall apart, about 20 minutes.

2. Top the potato slices with the cod fillets and add the clam juice. Increase the heat to medium-high and bring the liquid to a simmer. Cover the skillet, reduce the heat to very low, and poach the fish until it just flakes when tested with a fork, 5 to 7 minutes. Transfer the fish to a serving platter and cover loosely with foil to keep warm.

3. Increase the heat under the skillet to high and cook, whisking occasionally, until the liquid is reduced by half, 6 to 7 minutes. Remove the skillet from the heat, add the garlic, parsley, and pepper, and whisk until combined. Spoon the potato sauce over the fish and serve hot.

KITCHEN NOTE: *In order for the potatoes to cook down and become the sauce in this Basque-style dish, they must be cut as thin as possible. If you do not have a box-style vegetable slicer with adjustable settings, try cutting the potatoes with a swivel-bladed vegetable peeler.*

Poached Salmon in Orange-Lemon Sauce

SERVES 4

¾ CUP BOTTLED CLAM JUICE OR
    REDUCED-SODIUM CHICKEN BROTH
¾ CUP DRY WHITE WINE
⅔ CUP ORANGE JUICE
1 TABLESPOON FRESH LEMON JUICE
2 SHALLOTS, FINELY CHOPPED
1 TABLESPOON FRESH THYME, OR 1
    TEASPOON DRIED

¼ TEASPOON BLACK PEPPER
1 POUND SALMON FILLETS, SLICED
    HORIZONTALLY INTO 4 SERVING
    PIECES
2 TABLESPOONS UNSALTED BUTTER
1 LARGE HEAD OF BOSTON LETTUCE,
    SEPARATED INTO LEAVES
¼ TEASPOON SALT

1. In a large skillet, combine the clam juice, wine, orange juice, lemon juice, half of the shallots, half of the thyme, and ⅛ teaspoon of the pepper. Bring to a boil, then reduce the heat to medium-low and simmer the liquid for 10 minutes.

2. If some of the pieces of fish are thicker than the others, place them in the poaching liquid first and cook for about 1 minute. Add the thinner pieces and continue poaching the fish until it is opaque and feels firm to the touch, 3 to 4 minutes. Transfer the fish to a plate; cover loosely with foil to keep warm.

3. Increase the heat to medium and simmer the poaching liquid until it is reduced to about ½ cup. Strain the sauce through a sieve into a small pan and set aside.

4. Melt 1 tablespoon of the butter in the same skillet over medium heat. Add the remaining shallots and thyme, and cook them for 1 minute, stirring. Add the lettuce leaves, ⅛ teaspoon of the salt, and the remaining ⅛ teaspoon pepper. Cook the lettuce, stirring, until it has wilted, about 2 minutes. Place the lettuce on a platter.

5. Reheat the sauce; stir in the remaining ⅛ teaspoon salt and whisk in the remaining 1 tablespoon butter. Put the fish pieces on the lettuce, pour the sauce over the fish, and serve hot.

RED SNAPPER WITH VEGETABLE JULIENNE

SERVES 4

1½ CUPS CHICKEN BROTH, PREFERABLY REDUCED-SODIUM

¼ CUP DRY WHITE WINE OR CHICKEN BROTH

¼ TEASPOON BLACK PEPPER

1 BAY LEAF

1 SMALL ONION, QUARTERED

4 SMALL RED SNAPPER FILLETS (ABOUT 1¼ POUNDS TOTAL)

2 CELERY RIBS, CUT INTO 3-INCH-LONG MATCHSTICKS

1 MEDIUM YELLOW OR GREEN BELL PEPPER, CUT INTO THIN STRIPS

1 LARGE LEEK, WHITE AND TENDER GREEN PARTS ONLY, CUT INTO 3-INCH-LONG MATCHSTICKS

1 LARGE CARROT, CUT INTO 3-INCH-LONG MATCHSTICKS

2 TABLESPOONS CORNSTARCH BLENDED WITH 3 TABLESPOONS MILK

1. In a large skillet, bring the broth, wine, black pepper, bay leaf, and onion quarters to a boil over medium-high heat. Add the fish, reduce the heat to low, cover, and simmer until the fish just flakes when tested with a fork, about 10 minutes. With a slotted spatula, carefully remove the fish to a plate and cover loosely with foil to keep warm.

2. Discard the bay leaf. Bring the broth to a boil over medium-high heat and cook uncovered to reduce it to 1 cup, about 5 minutes.

3. Add the celery, bell pepper, leek, and carrot, reduce the heat to low, cover, and simmer until the vegetables are crisp-tender, about 11 minutes.

4. Return the broth to a boil over medium-high heat and stir in the cornstarch mixture. Cook until thickened slightly, 1 to 2 minutes.

5. Serve the fish topped with the sauce and vegetables.

POACHED SALMON WITH DILL BUTTER

SERVES 4

1 LEMON, HALVED

4 SALMON STEAKS (1 INCH THICK, ABOUT 2 POUNDS TOTAL)

8 SCALLIONS, TRIMMED BUT LEFT WHOLE

8 FRESH DILL SPRIGS (OPTIONAL)

4 TABLESPOONS UNSALTED BUTTER, AT ROOM TEMPERATURE

2 TABLESPOONS MINCED FRESH DILL, OR ¾ TEASPOON DRIED

½ TEASPOON SALT

⅛ TEASPOON BLACK PEPPER

1. In a large skillet, bring 2 inches of water to a boil. Add the lemon halves and reduce the heat so that the water just simmers.

2. Add the salmon steaks (if they do not fit in a single layer, cook them in two batches), scallions, and dill sprigs (if using). The fish should be completely covered by the water; add more water if necessary. When the water returns to a simmer (do not let the water boil), cook the salmon until it is firm and light pink in the center, 8 to 10 minutes.

3. Meanwhile, in a small bowl, beat the butter until creamy and smooth. Beat in the minced dill, salt, and pepper.

4. Transfer the salmon to a serving platter or individual plates. Top each steak with one-fourth of the dill butter and two of the poached scallions.

Variation: *Although dill and salmon are natural partners, there are a number of fresh herbs that would go well with the rich taste of this fish. Try basil (same quantities as for the dill) or tarragon (use 2 teaspoons minced fresh or ½ teaspoon dried).*

Salmon with Dill Sauce

SERVES 4

◆ EXTRA-QUICK

3 CUPS CHICKEN BROTH, PREFERABLY
   REDUCED-SODIUM

3 GARLIC CLOVES, PEELED

3 SCALLIONS, TRIMMED BUT LEFT
   WHOLE

2 CUPS (PACKED) FRESH SPINACH
   LEAVES, OR ¼ CUP FROZEN
   SPINACH, THAWED

¼ CUP (PACKED) FRESH DILL SPRIGS,
   OR 1½ TEASPOONS DRIED

3 TABLESPOONS FRESH LEMON JUICE

4 SMALL SALMON STEAKS (ABOUT 1¾
   POUNDS TOTAL)

2 TABLESPOONS UNSALTED BUTTER

1 TABLESPOON DIJON MUSTARD

1½ TEASPOONS GRATED LEMON ZEST

¼ TEASPOON SALT

¼ TEASPOON BLACK PEPPER

½ CUP SOUR CREAM

1. In a large skillet, bring the broth and whole garlic cloves to a boil over medium-high heat.

2. Add the scallions, spinach, dill, lemon juice, and salmon steaks to the boiling broth. Reduce the heat to low, cover, and simmer until the salmon just flakes when tested with a fork, 5 to 7 minutes. Transfer the salmon steaks to a plate and cover loosely with foil to keep warm.

3. With a slotted spoon, transfer the garlic, scallions, spinach, and dill to a food processor (reserve the broth for another use, if desired). Purée the cooked vegetables in the food processor. Add the butter, mustard, lemon zest, salt, and pepper. Add the sour cream to the sauce and process to blend.

4. Serve the steaks topped with some of the sauce.

Tex-Mex Steamed Swordfish

SERVES 4

◆ EXTRA-QUICK ◇ LOW-FAT

2 LARGE SWORDFISH STEAKS (¾ INCH THICK, ABOUT 1¼ POUNDS TOTAL)

2 CUPS SHREDDED CABBAGE

1 LARGE YELLOW OR RED BELL PEPPER, CUT INTO THIN RINGS

1 MEDIUM RED ONION, CUT INTO THIN RINGS

2 LIMES

1½ TABLESPOONS UNSALTED BUTTER, MELTED

1 TEASPOON CHILI POWDER

¾ TEASPOON CUMIN

¼ TEASPOON SALT

¼ TEASPOON BLACK PEPPER

PINCH OF CAYENNE PEPPER

8 CORN TORTILLAS, WRAPPED IN FOIL

1. Cut the swordfish steaks in half to make 4 equal serving portions.

2. Line a flat vegetable steamer or steamer insert with the shredded cabbage, bell pepper, and onion. Bring the water in the steamer to a boil and steam the vegetables for about 1 minute.

3. Meanwhile, grate the zest from one of the limes. Cut both limes into quarters.

4. In a small bowl, combine the melted butter, lime zest, chili powder, cumin, salt, black pepper, and cayenne.

5. Remove the steamer from the heat. Place the fish steaks on top of the steamed vegetables. Brush the fish with the seasoned butter. Re-cover and steam until the fish just flakes when tested with a fork, about 4 minutes.

6. Meanwhile, warm the tortillas in the oven or a toaster oven.

7. Dividing evenly, serve the fish with the steamed vegetables. Using one-quarter lime per portion, squeeze the lime juice over the fish. Serve with one lime wedge and two warm tortillas per person.

SWORDFISH AND LEEKS WITH BELL PEPPER PURÉE

SERVES 4

◇ LOW-FAT

2 LARGE SWORDFISH STEAKS (¾ INCH THICK, ABOUT 1¼ POUNDS TOTAL)

2 CUPS REDUCED-SODIUM CHICKEN BROTH

1 TEASPOON BALSAMIC VINEGAR OR CIDER VINEGAR

1½ TEASPOONS TARRAGON

½ TEASPOON BLACK PEPPER

1 BAY LEAF

2 MEDIUM LEEKS, CUT INTO 2½-INCH LENGTHS, OR 12 SCALLIONS, WHITE PARTS ONLY

1 LARGE RED BELL PEPPER, CUT INTO LARGE PIECES

1 LARGE YELLOW BELL PEPPER, CUT INTO LARGE PIECES

2 GARLIC CLOVES, PEELED

3 TABLESPOONS SOUR CREAM

1. Cut the swordfish steaks in half.

2. In a large skillet, bring the broth, vinegar, tarragon, pepper, and bay leaf to a boil over medium-high heat. Add the swordfish, leeks, bell peppers, and garlic, and return to a boil. Reduce the heat to medium-low, cover, and simmer until the swordfish just flakes when tested with a fork, about 6 minutes.

3. Remove the swordfish and leeks to a plate, cover loosely with foil, and set aside. Increase the heat under the skillet to high, bring the broth to a boil, and cook the peppers until tender, about 2 minutes. Discard the bay leaf.

4. With a slotted spoon, transfer the peppers and garlic to a food processor. Continue to boil the broth in the skillet until it is reduced to about ½ cup.

5. Meanwhile, process the peppers and garlic to a purée. When the broth has been reduced, add 2 tablespoons of it to the food processor along with the sour cream, and purée until smooth. (Discard any remaining broth.)

6. Serve the swordfish and leeks with the bell pepper purée.

Pan-Fried Halibut with Sweet-and-Sour Sauce

SERVES 4

4 TABLESPOONS CORNSTARCH

1 CUP PINEAPPLE JUICE

½ CUP PLUS 2 TEASPOONS VEGETABLE
OIL

3 GARLIC CLOVES, MINCED

6 QUARTER-SIZE SLICES FRESH GINGER,
COARSELY CHOPPED

4 SCALLIONS, COARSELY CHOPPED

¼ CUP CIDER VINEGAR

4 TEASPOONS REDUCED-SODIUM SOY
SAUCE

¼ CUP KETCHUP

4 TEASPOONS SUGAR

½ TEASPOON BLACK PEPPER

1 EGG WHITE

1¾ POUNDS HALIBUT STEAKS, CUT
INTO ½-INCH-WIDE STRIPS

½ CUP SESAME SEEDS

1. In a small bowl, combine 3 tablespoons of the cornstarch with the pineapple juice.

2. In a small skillet or saucepan, warm 2 teaspoons of the oil over medium-high heat. Add the garlic, ginger, and scallions, and cook, stirring, until the garlic begins to brown, about 3 minutes.

3. Add the cornstarch-pineapple juice mixture, the vinegar, 2 teaspoons of the soy sauce, the ketchup, sugar, and pepper, and bring to a boil over medium-high heat. Reduce the heat to low, cover, and simmer while you prepare the fish.

4. In a shallow bowl, beat the egg white with the remaining 1 tablespoon cornstarch and 2 teaspoons soy sauce. Add the fish to the egg white mixture and toss to coat well. Place the fish strips on a plate and sprinkle them with the sesame seeds, turning the fish to coat all sides.

5. In a medium nonstick skillet, warm the remaining ½ cup oil over medium-high heat. Add the fish in batches and cook until golden, about 3 minutes per side. As they are done, place the fish on a paper towel-lined plate in a low oven to keep warm.

6. Serve the fish with the hot sweet-and-sour sauce on the side.

BREADED FISH WITH LEMON BUTTER

SERVES 4

1 CUP FINE UNSEASONED DRY BREAD
CRUMBS

½ CUP FLOUR

2 EGGS

1½ POUNDS FLOUNDER OR SOLE
FILLETS

1½ STICKS UNSALTED BUTTER, AT
ROOM TEMPERATURE

¼ CUP FRESH LEMON JUICE

½ TEASPOON CELERY SEED

PINCH OF GROUND CLOVES

¼ TEASPOON SALT

¼ TEASPOON BLACK PEPPER

1 TABLESPOON VEGETABLE OIL

1. Place the bread crumbs and flour in separate shallow bowls or pie plates. Break the eggs into another shallow bowl and beat with a fork. One at a time, dip the fillets in the flour, coating both sides. Gently shake off the excess and dip into the egg. Let the excess drain off and dip the fillet in the bread crumbs, coating both sides. Place the fish on a plate, cover, and chill until ready to proceed.

2. In a medium bowl, beat 1 stick of the butter until well softened. Add the lemon juice, celery seed, cloves, salt, and pepper, and beat until blended. Transfer the sauce to a small serving bowl.

3. In a large nonstick skillet, warm the oil with 2 tablespoons of the butter over medium-high heat. When the butter and oil begin to foam, add the fillets and reduce the heat to medium. Cook until the fillets are golden brown, about 3 minutes per side. Add the remaining 2 tablespoons butter as necessary. Transfer the fillets to paper towels to drain.

4. Arrange the fillets on a serving platter. Serve hot with the lemon butter on the side.

Sautéed Sesame Fish

SERVES 4

◆ EXTRA-QUICK

¼ CUP FLOUR

1 TEASPOON SALT

¼ TEASPOON BLACK PEPPER

4 FIRM HALIBUT, SEA BASS, OR RED
SNAPPER FILLETS (¾ TO 1 INCH
THICK, ABOUT 2 POUNDS TOTAL)

⅔ CUP FINE UNSEASONED DRY BREAD
CRUMBS

¼ CUP SESAME SEEDS

1 EGG

1 TABLESPOON MILK

2 TABLESPOONS VEGETABLE OIL

2 TABLESPOONS UNSALTED BUTTER

1 LEMON, CUT INTO 8 WEDGES

1. In a bowl, combine the flour, salt, and pepper. Dredge the fish lightly in the seasoned flour.

2. In a shallow bowl, combine the bread crumbs and sesame seeds. In another shallow bowl, blend the egg with the milk.

3. Dip the fish into the egg mixture, then into the bread crumb mixture, turning to coat the fish completely.

4. In a large skillet, warm the oil with the butter over medium-high heat. When the butter and oil begin to foam, add the fish steaks and cook them until golden brown, about 5 minutes per side.

5. Serve the fish hot with the lemon wedges.

KITCHEN NOTE: *Sesame seeds are basic to a number of cuisines, including those of Africa, the Middle East, India, and China. You can buy hulled or unhulled sesame seeds, though the most common supermarket variety is the lighter colored hulled type. The darker unhulled sesame seeds still have the bran intact and are an excellent source of calcium, iron, and phosphorous.*

Shallow-Fried Fish Tempura with Two Sauces

SERVES 4

3 TABLESPOONS REDUCED-SODIUM SOY
 SAUCE
2 TABLESPOONS CIDER VINEGAR
1½ TEASPOONS ORIENTAL (DARK)
 SESAME OIL
2 QUARTER-SIZE SLICES FRESH GINGER,
 MINCED
⅛ TEASPOON RED PEPPER FLAKES
½ TEASPOON BLACK PEPPER
¼ CUP MAYONNAISE

¼ CUP PLAIN LOW-FAT YOGURT
3 TABLESPOONS PICKLE RELISH
⅓ CUP CORNSTARCH
2 TABLESPOONS FLOUR
½ TEASPOON BAKING POWDER
½ TEASPOON SALT
1 EGG
1 CUP VEGETABLE OIL
1 POUND COD OR GROUPER FILLETS,
 CUT INTO 1½-INCH CHUNKS

1. In a small bowl, combine the soy sauce, vinegar, sesame oil, ginger, red pepper flakes, and ⅛ teaspoon of the black pepper. Set the ginger-soy sauce aside.

2. In another small bowl, combine the mayonnaise, yogurt, pickle relish, and ⅛ teaspoon of the black pepper. Refrigerate the tartar sauce until serving time.

3. In a medium bowl, combine the cornstarch, flour, baking powder, salt, and the remaining ¼ teaspoon black pepper. In a small bowl, beat the egg with 2 tablespoons of water. Stir the egg mixture into the dry ingredients and beat to blend.

4. In a small saucepan, warm the oil until it shimmers but is not smoking.

5. Meanwhile, dip the fish in the batter. When the oil is hot, add the fish in batches, without crowding, and cook until golden brown, about 3 minutes, turning the fish over once or twice as it cooks. Remove the fish chunks with a slotted spoon and drain them on paper towels. Keep the fish warm in a low oven while you cook the remaining batches.

6. Serve the fish with the sauces on the side.

SAUTÉED CURRIED GROUPER

SERVES 4

◆ EXTRA-QUICK ◇ LOW-FAT

1 POUND GROUPER, RED SNAPPER, OR
   SEA BASS FILLETS

3 TABLESPOONS FRESH LIME JUICE

2 TABLESPOONS VEGETABLE OIL

1 TABLESPOON CURRY POWDER

½ TEASPOON BLACK PEPPER

1 LARGE RED APPLE, CUT INTO PIECES

¾ CUP CHOPPED ONION

1 TEASPOON FENNEL SEEDS, CRUSHED

¼ TEASPOON SALT

1 CUP FROZEN PEAS, THAWED

¼ CUP DRY WHITE WINE

1. Cut the fish into 1-inch pieces.

2. In a small bowl, combine the lime juice, 1 tablespoon of the oil, the curry powder, and pepper. Put the fish pieces, apple, onion, and fennel seeds into a large bowl. Pour the curry mixture over the fish and mix well. Let the fish marinate for 10 minutes.

3. In a large skillet, warm the remaining 1 tablespoon oil over high heat. When the oil is

hot, add the fish mixture and marinade. Sprinkle in the salt and cook the curry for 3 minutes, stirring constantly.

4. Add the peas and white wine, and cook the curry, stirring often, until the fish is firm to the touch, 2 to 3 minutes. Serve the curried fish hot.

VARIATION: *For a fish dish with Mexican flair, use chili powder in place of the curry powder and cumin seed (or ground cumin) in place of the fennel. For extra depth of flavor, toast the cumin in a dry skillet first. Serve the dish sprinkled with chopped cilantro.*

Pan-Fried Haddock with Spanish Vegetables

SERVES 4

½ CUP PLUS 2 TABLESPOONS OLIVE OIL

2 MEDIUM ONIONS, MINCED

1 LARGE GREEN BELL PEPPER, MINCED

1 SMALL RED BELL PEPPER, MINCED

⅔ CUP FINELY CHOPPED SMOKED HAM

¼ CUP CHOPPED PARSLEY

¼ CUP DRY SHERRY

1½ TABLESPOONS PAPRIKA

¼ TEASPOON BLACK PEPPER

⅓ CUP FLOUR

4 HADDOCK STEAKS (1¼ INCHES THICK, ABOUT 2 POUNDS TOTAL)

1 TEASPOON MINCED GARLIC

1 PIMIENTO, CUT INTO 4 STRIPS (OPTIONAL)

4 PITTED BLACK OLIVES (OPTIONAL)

1. In a large skillet, warm 2 tablespoons of the oil over medium heat. Add the onions and bell peppers, and cook until the vegetables are softened, 2 to 3 minutes. Add the ham and cook until it just begins to brown, about 3 minutes.

2. Stir in the parsley, sherry, paprika, black pepper, and ⅓ cup of water. Bring the mixture to a simmer and cook over low heat, partially covered, until the mixture softens to a marmalade consistency, about 20 minutes.

3. Meanwhile, place the flour on a sheet of wax paper.

4. Pour the remaining ½ cup oil into a large skillet (it should come to a depth of at least ¼ inch). Warm the oil over medium-high heat. Dredge the haddock steaks in the flour. Carefully place the fish in the skillet and fry, turning several times, until it is browned and just flakes when tested with a fork, 10 to 15 minutes. Transfer the fish to paper towels to drain briefly.

5. To serve, stir the minced garlic into the vegetable mixture and divide among 4 dinner plates. Arrange the steaks on top and garnish with pimiento strips and olives, if desired.

49

Monkfish Provençale

SERVES 4

¼ CUP FLOUR

2 TABLESPOONS OLIVE OIL

2 POUNDS MONKFISH FILLETS, CUT ON
THE DIAGONAL INTO THICK SLICES

4 TABLESPOONS UNSALTED BUTTER

3 TABLESPOONS MINCED SHALLOTS OR
ONION

1 TEASPOON MINCED GARLIC

¾ CUP MINCED PARSLEY

4 CUPS CHOPPED FRESH OR CANNED
TOMATOES

½ TEASPOON SALT

¼ TEASPOON BLACK PEPPER

1. Place the flour in a shallow bowl or pie plate.

2. In a large skillet, warm the oil over high heat. Working quickly, lightly dredge each piece of fish in the flour and add to the skillet. Fry until golden brown, about 1½ minutes per side. Transfer the monkfish to a platter and cover loosely with foil to keep warm.

3. Pour off the oil from the skillet, add the butter, and warm over medium-high heat until the butter starts to sizzle. Add shallots, garlic, parsley, tomatoes, and any juices that have collected under the fish, and stir to combine. Stir in the salt and pepper.

4. Divide the sauce among 4 dinner plates, top with fish, and serve hot.

KITCHEN NOTE: *Monkfish is an exceptionally firm fish whose texture is often compared with lobster. Also like lobster, monkfish can get quite tough if cooked for too long. To avoid this problem, the monkfish fillets for this recipe are cut into slices so that they can be quickly cooked—only a total of 3 minutes.*

SALMON PATTIES WITH CITRUS VINAIGRETTE

SERVES 4

1 ORANGE

1 LEMON

¼ CUP OLIVE OIL

2 TEASPOONS REDUCED-SODIUM SOY
SAUCE

2 DROPS OF HOT PEPPER SAUCE

6 QUARTER-SIZE SLICES FRESH GINGER,
MINCED

⅓ CUP (PACKED) CILANTRO SPRIGS,
MINCED

ONE 14¾-OUNCE CAN SALMON,
DRAINED

3 SCALLIONS, MINCED

1 CUP FINE UNSEASONED DRY BREAD
CRUMBS

2 EGGS

1 TEASPOON DRY MUSTARD

¼ TEASPOON BLACK PEPPER

1. Grate the orange and the lemon to yield 2 teaspoons each of zest. Halve the orange and lemon, then juice one orange half and one lemon half. Remove the peel and as much of the bitter white pith as possible from the un-juiced orange and lemon halves. Cut the peeled orange and lemon into bite-size pieces.

2. In a small bowl, combine the orange and lemon zests, juices, and pieces. Stir in 2 table-spoons of the oil, the soy sauce, hot pepper sauce, and half of the ginger and cilantro.

3. In a medium bowl, combine the salmon, scallions, and the remaining ginger and cilantro, and toss to break up the salmon and distribute the ingredients.

4. Add the bread crumbs, eggs, mustard, and pepper, and thoroughly combine. Form the mixture into 4 patties about 4 inches across.

5. In a large skillet, warm 1 tablespoon of the oil over medium-high heat. Add the salmon patties and cook until golden on one side, about 3 minutes. Turn the patties over, add the remaining 1 tablespoon oil, and cook until golden on the second side, about 3 min-utes. Serve the patties with the sauce on the side.

Salmon with Fresh Basil Sauce

SERVES 4

1 POUND SALMON FILLETS

1 TABLESPOON OLIVE OIL

1½ TABLESPOONS FRESH LEMON JUICE

¼ TEASPOON SALT

¼ TEASPOON BLACK PEPPER

2 SHALLOTS OR SCALLIONS, THINLY
   SLICED

1 GARLIC CLOVE, MINCED

2 CUPS (LOOSELY PACKED) BASIL
   LEAVES

¼ CUP FISH BROTH, BOTTLED CLAM
   JUICE, OR DRY WHITE WINE

¼ CUP HEAVY CREAM

1. Cut the fish diagonally across the grain into slices about 1 inch thick.

2. In a large skillet, warm the oil over high heat. Add the fish pieces and cook for 3 minutes. Carefully turn the fish over and sprinkle them with the lemon juice and ⅛ teaspoon each of the salt and pepper. Cook until the fish just flakes when tested with a fork, about 3 minutes. Transfer the fish to a serving platter and cover loosely with foil to keep warm.

3. Return the skillet to medium heat. Add the shallots and garlic, and cook, stirring constantly, for 30 seconds. Add the basil and broth, and simmer the mixture for 1 minute.

4. Stir in the cream and the remaining ⅛ teaspoon each salt and pepper, and simmer the sauce until it thickens slightly, about 2 minutes. Pour the sauce over the fish and serve hot.

Sweet Afterthought: *To follow this rich main dish, offer a bowl of perfect whole strawberries that you've sprinkled with balsamic vinegar. This very special aged red wine vinegar from Italy is mild and mellow, and it brings out the sweetness of the berries.*

Corn-Fried Snapper with Spicy Pineapple Salsa

SERVES 4

♦ EXTRA-QUICK

⅓ CUP CORNMEAL

2 TABLESPOONS CHOPPED PARSLEY
   (OPTIONAL)

1 TEASPOON CUMIN

¾ TEASPOON SALT

¼ TEASPOON CAYENNE PEPPER

1 EGG WHITE

4 RED SNAPPER FILLETS (ABOUT 1¼
   POUNDS TOTAL)

2 TABLESPOONS PLUS 1 TEASPOON
   OLIVE OIL

1 TABLESPOON UNSALTED BUTTER

1 PLUM TOMATO, MINCED

1 FRESH OR PICKLED JALAPEÑO PEPPER,
   SEEDED AND MINCED

2 TABLESPOONS CHOPPED FRESH MINT,
   OR 1 TEASPOON DRIED

ONE 8-OUNCE CAN JUICE-PACKED
   CRUSHED PINEAPPLE, DRAINED

2 TEASPOONS FRESH LIME JUICE

1 TEASPOON GRATED LIME ZEST
   (OPTIONAL)

1. In a shallow bowl, combine the cornmeal, parsley (if using), cumin, ½ teaspoon of the salt, and the cayenne. In another shallow bowl, lightly beat the egg white. Dip the fish in the egg white and then in the cornmeal mixture.

2. In a large nonstick skillet, warm 2 tablespoons of the oil with the butter over medium-high heat until the butter is melted. Add the fish and cook until it just flakes when tested with a fork and is golden brown on both sides, 3 to 4 minutes per side.

3. Meanwhile, in a small bowl, combine the tomato, jalapeño, mint, pineapple, lime juice, lime zest (if using), and the remaining 1 teaspoon oil and ¼ teaspoon salt.

4. Serve the fish topped with the pineapple salsa.

PECAN-CRUSTED SNAPPER WITH SCALLIONS

SERVES 4

♦ EXTRA-QUICK

2 SCALLIONS, MINCED

½ CUP FINELY CHOPPED PECANS

2 TABLESPOONS FINE UNSEASONED DRY
   BREAD CRUMBS

¼ CUP FLOUR

1 TEASPOON SALT

½ TEASPOON BLACK PEPPER

1 EGG

1 TABLESPOON MILK

4 RED SNAPPER FILLETS (ABOUT
   1 POUND TOTAL)

1 TABLESPOON VEGETABLE OIL

2 TABLESPOONS UNSALTED BUTTER

1. In a shallow bowl, combine the scallions, pecans, and bread crumbs. In another shallow bowl, combine the flour, salt, and pepper. In a third shallow bowl, blend the egg and milk.

2. Dredge the fish in the flour mixture, then in the egg, and finally in the pecan mixture.

3. In a large skillet, preferably nonstick, warm the oil with 1 tablespoon of the butter over medium-high heat until the butter is melted. Add the fish and cook until golden on the bottom, about 3 minutes.

4. Carefully turn the fish, add the remaining 1 tablespoon butter, and cook until the fish is golden on the second side and just flakes when tested with a fork, about 3 minutes.

VARIATION: *The richness of nuts is well matched to the mild flavors of most fish. Try this dish with hazelnuts, walnuts, almonds, or unsalted pistachios.*

RED SNAPPER
WITH TOASTED ALMONDS

SERVES 4

⅓ CUP SLICED ALMONDS

3 TABLESPOONS FLOUR

½ TEASPOON SALT

¼ TEASPOON BLACK PEPPER

1¾ POUNDS RED SNAPPER FILLETS

1 TABLESPOON VEGETABLE OIL

3 TABLESPOONS UNSALTED BUTTER

4 SCALLIONS, COARSELY CHOPPED

2 GARLIC CLOVES, MINCED

1. In a large ungreased skillet, toast the almonds over medium heat, shaking frequently, until golden, about 5 minutes. Remove the almonds from the pan and set aside.

2. In a shallow bowl, combine the flour, salt, and pepper. Lightly dredge the snapper fillets in the seasoned flour.

3. In the same large skillet, warm the oil with 1 tablespoon of the butter over medium-high heat until the butter is melted. Add the fillets and sauté until golden brown and cooked through, about 4 minutes per side. Remove the fish to a plate and cover loosely to keep warm.

4. Add the remaining 2 tablespoons butter to the skillet. Add the scallions and garlic, and sauté until the scallions are just limp, about 1 minute. Add the almonds and cook until coated with butter, about 1 minute.

5. Serve the fish topped with the almonds and scallions.

Red Snapper with Spicy Orange Sauce

SERVES 4

♦ EXTRA - QUICK

2 RED SNAPPER FILLETS (ABOUT 1¼
    POUNDS TOTAL)

2 TABLESPOONS FLOUR

¾ TEASPOON SALT

⅜ TEASPOON BLACK PEPPER

1 TABLESPOON OLIVE OIL

4 TABLESPOONS UNSALTED BUTTER, AT
    ROOM TEMPERATURE

1 TABLESPOON FROZEN ORANGE JUICE
    CONCENTRATE

1 TEASPOON CHILI POWDER

2 TABLESPOONS CHOPPED PARSLEY

1. Cut each fish fillet in half to make 4 equal servings.

2. In a shallow bowl, combine the flour, ½ teaspoon of the salt, and ¼ teaspoon of the pepper. Dredge the fish lightly in the seasoned flour.

3. In a large skillet, preferably nonstick, warm the oil over medium-high heat. Add the fish and cook, turning once, until the fish just flakes when tested with a fork, 6 to 8 minutes.

4. Meanwhile, in a small bowl, blend the butter, orange juice concentrate, chili powder, and the remaining ¼ teaspoon salt and ⅛ teaspoon pepper.

5. Transfer the fish to dinner plates and top each serving with 1 tablespoon of the spicy orange sauce. Sprinkle with the parsley and serve hot.

Mexican-Style Sole with Almonds

SERVES 4

1 CUP SLICED ALMONDS

1½ POUNDS SOLE OR FLOUNDER
  FILLETS

¼ TEASPOON SALT

¼ TEASPOON BLACK PEPPER

2 EGGS

2 TABLESPOONS OLIVE OIL

3 TABLESPOONS UNSALTED BUTTER

½ CUP CHOPPED ONION

1 LARGE GARLIC CLOVE, MINCED

ONE 4-OUNCE CAN CHOPPED MILD
  GREEN CHILIES, RINSED AND
  DRAINED

2 TABLESPOONS FRESH LIME JUICE

1 TABLESPOON GRATED LIME ZEST

¼ CUP CHOPPED CILANTRO

1. Preheat the oven to 350°. Place the almonds on a baking sheet and bake for 5 to 8 minutes, or until toasted. Remove the almonds and set aside. Reduce the oven temperature to 250°.

2. Sprinkle the fish with the salt and pepper. Break the eggs into a shallow bowl and beat lightly.

3. In a large skillet, warm the oil with the butter over medium-high heat until the butter is melted. Dip half of the fillets in the beaten egg. Add to the skillet and cook until the egg is set and golden, 2 to 3 minutes per side.

Transfer the fish to a platter and keep warm in the oven. Repeat with the remaining fillets.

4. Add the onion, garlic, and chilies to the skillet, and sauté, stirring, for 1 minute. Add the lime juice, lime zest, and cilantro, and stir to combine.

5. Spoon the sauce over the fish, then sprinkle with the toasted almonds. Serve hot.

Sole with Tomato-Basil Sauce

SERVES 4

¼ CUP PLUS 2 TABLESPOONS OLIVE OIL

2 GARLIC CLOVES, MINCED

1½ CUPS CHOPPED CANNED TOMATOES

½ CUP DRY WHITE WINE OR DRY
    VERMOUTH

3 TABLESPOONS CHOPPED FRESH BASIL,
    OR 2 TEASPOONS DRIED

2 TABLESPOONS CAPERS

¼ TEASPOON SALT

¼ TEASPOON BLACK PEPPER

¾ CUP FLOUR

4 SOLE OR FLOUNDER FILLETS (ABOUT
    1½ POUNDS TOTAL)

⅓ CUP GRATED PARMESAN CHEESE

½ CUP PITTED BLACK OLIVES, SLIVERED

1. In a medium skillet, heat 2 tablespoons of the oil over medium-high heat. Add the garlic and sauté until golden, 2 to 3 minutes.

2. Add the tomatoes, wine, basil, and capers to the skillet, and stir to combine. Increase the heat to high and quickly bring the sauce to a boil. Immediately remove the skillet from the heat, stir in the salt and pepper, and set aside.

3. Place the flour on a sheet of wax paper. Dredge the fillets well in the flour; shake off the excess.

4. In a large skillet, heat the remaining ¼ cup oil over medium-high heat. Add the fillets, arranging them in a single layer, and lightly brown on one side, about 4 minutes. Turn the fish and brown on the second side, about 4 minutes.

5. Return the sauce to medium heat and cook until reheated, 2 to 3 minutes. Divide the fish among dinner plates. Top each fillet with hot tomato sauce, sprinkle with the Parmesan, and top with the olives.

BROOK TROUT WITH MUSHROOM SAUCE

SERVES 4

8 BROOK TROUT, RAINBOW TROUT, OR
   PERCH FILLETS
½ CUP FRESH LEMON JUICE
7 TABLESPOONS UNSALTED BUTTER
1 GARLIC CLOVE, LIGHTLY CRUSHED
   AND PEELED
1 POUND SMALL MUSHROOMS, THINLY
   SLICED

1 CUP DRY WHITE WINE
1 CUP HEAVY CREAM
1 TEASPOON SALT
1 TEASPOON BLACK PEPPER
1 CUP FLOUR
1 TEASPOON FRESH THYME, OR
   ¼ TEASPOON DRIED

1. Arrange the fish in a single layer in a shallow container. Pour the lemon juice over the fish and set aside to marinate.

2. In a medium saucepan, warm 3 tablespoons of the butter over medium heat until it is melted. Add the garlic and sauté, stirring, for 1 minute. Remove the garlic and discard. Add the mushrooms and cook, stirring, until the liquid has almost evaporated, about 10 minutes.

3. Increase the heat to medium-high. Add the wine and cook, stirring often, until the liquid has reduced by half, about 5 minutes.

4. Add the heavy cream and cook, stirring, over medium heat until the sauce has thickened slightly, 3 to 4 minutes. Do not boil. Add ¼ teaspoon each of the salt and pepper.

Keep the mushroom sauce warm over very low heat until ready to use.

5. In a shallow bowl or pie plate, combine the flour, thyme, and remaining ¾ teaspoon each salt and pepper.

6. In a large skillet, warm 2 tablespoons of the butter over medium heat until lightly browned. Meanwhile, dredge 4 fillets in the seasoned flour. Add the fillets to the skillet and cook until golden brown, about 2 minutes per side. Transfer the fillets to a paper towel-lined plate to drain; cover loosely with foil to keep warm. Repeat the process for the remaining fillets, using the remaining 2 tablespoons butter.

7. Spoon the mushroom sauce over the fish and serve hot.

59

SWORDFISH PICCATA

SERVES 4

◆ EXTRA-QUICK

¼ CUP FLOUR

½ TEASPOON SALT

¼ TEASPOON BLACK PEPPER

1 POUND SWORDFISH STEAKS (¾ INCH THICK), CUT INTO ½-INCH-WIDE STRIPS

2 TABLESPOONS OLIVE OIL

2 TABLESPOONS UNSALTED BUTTER

3 LARGE SHALLOTS, HALVED, OR 1 SMALL ONION, QUARTERED

2 GARLIC CLOVES, MINCED

⅓ CUP CHICKEN BROTH

2 TABLESPOONS FRESH LEMON JUICE

¼ CUP CHOPPED FRESH DILL, OR 1 TABLESPOON DRIED

1 TABLESPOON GRATED LEMON ZEST (OPTIONAL)

1. In a plastic or paper bag, combine the flour, salt, and pepper, and shake to mix. Add the swordfish and shake to coat lightly. Remove the fish and set aside.

2. In a large skillet, preferably nonstick, warm the oil with the butter over medium-high heat until the butter is melted. Add the shallots and garlic, and sauté until the shallots are translucent, about 3 minutes.

3. Add the swordfish strips and cook, turning them carefully, until the fish is medium-rare, about 4 minutes.

4. Stir in the broth, lemon juice, dill, and lemon zest (if using). Bring the mixture to a boil, remove from the heat, and serve hot.

VARIATION: *For a dish with a similar rich flavor and meaty texture, substitute tuna for the swordfish. The cooking time will be approximately the same.*

CRAB CAKES WITH QUICK RÉMOULADE SAUCE

SERVES 4

◆ EXTRA-QUICK

½ POUND HADDOCK, FLOUNDER, OR
   SOLE FILLETS

3 TABLESPOONS OLIVE OIL

ONE 6-OUNCE CAN CRABMEAT

2 EGGS, LIGHTLY BEATEN

5 TABLESPOONS REDUCED-FAT
   MAYONNAISE

5 TABLESPOONS DIJON MUSTARD

1 CUP FINE UNSEASONED DRY BREAD
   CRUMBS

¼ TEASPOON BLACK PEPPER

PINCH OF CAYENNE PEPPER

8 SCALLIONS, COARSELY CHOPPED

2 TABLESPOONS UNSALTED BUTTER

½ CUP PICKLE RELISH

1¼ TEASPOONS TARRAGON

1. Preheat the oven to 375°. Line a baking pan with foil. Place the fish in the pan and brush with 1 tablespoon of the oil. Bake until opaque throughout, about 8 minutes. Remove and let cool slightly.

2. In a medium bowl, combine the crabmeat with the eggs, 2 tablespoons of the mayonnaise, 2 tablespoons of the mustard, ½ cup of the bread crumbs, the black pepper, and cayenne. Stir in the scallions.

3. Flake the fish and combine it with the crabmeat mixture. Form the mixture into patties about 3½ inches in diameter and ½ inch thick and dredge them in the remaining ½ cup bread crumbs.

4. In a medium skillet, warm 1 tablespoon of the oil with 1 tablespoon of the butter over medium-high heat until the butter melts. Add the fish cakes and fry until golden all over, 2 to 3 minutes per side, turning carefully. Add the remaining 1 tablespoon each butter and oil as necessary to prevent sticking.

5. In a small bowl, combine the pickle relish, tarragon, and the remaining 3 tablespoons each mayonnaise and mustard.

6. Serve the fish cakes with the rémoulade sauce on the side.

LEMON SCALLOPS
WITH GREEN BEANS

SERVES 4

◆ EXTRA-QUICK ◇ LOW-FAT

½ CUP REDUCED-SODIUM CHICKEN
BROTH

1 TABLESPOON FRESH LEMON JUICE

2 TEASPOONS CORNSTARCH

1 TABLESPOON GRATED LEMON ZEST

½ TEASPOON BASIL

¼ TEASPOON BLACK PEPPER

1 TABLESPOON OLIVE OIL

1 SMALL RED ONION, CUT INTO THIN
WEDGES

2 GARLIC CLOVES, MINCED

¾ POUND SEA SCALLOPS, HALVED IF
LARGE

½ POUND FRESH GREEN BEANS, CUT
INTO 2-INCH LENGTHS, OR ONE
10-OUNCE PACKAGE FROZEN CUT
GREEN BEANS

1. In a small bowl, combine the chicken broth, lemon juice, cornstarch, lemon zest, basil, and pepper.

2. In a medium skillet, warm the oil over medium-high heat. Add the onion and garlic, and sauté for 1 minute. Add the scallops and cook until almost completely opaque, about 4 minutes.

3. Add the green beans. Stir the broth mixture to reblend the cornstarch and add it to the skillet. Bring the liquid to a boil, stirring constantly. Reduce the heat to medium-low, cover, and simmer until the beans are crisp-tender and the scallops are cooked through, about 4 minutes.

VARIATION: *Celebrate the arrival of summer by replacing the green beans with fresh sugar-snap peas. Pinch off the tips of the pods and pull off the strings, but leave the pods whole.*

SCALLOP-ASPARAGUS STIR-FRY WITH CURRIED RICE

SERVES 4

◇ LOW-FAT

1 TABLESPOON VEGETABLE OIL

1 SMALL ONION, COARSELY CHOPPED

3 TABLESPOONS CURRY POWDER

1 CUP RICE

1¼ CUPS CHICKEN BROTH

¼ TEASPOON SALT

¼ TEASPOON SUGAR

2 TABLESPOONS ORIENTAL (DARK)
   SESAME OIL

3 GARLIC CLOVES, MINCED

4 SCALLIONS, THICKLY SLICED

1 TABLESPOON MINCED FRESH GINGER

3 TABLESPOONS CORNSTARCH

¼ TEASPOON BLACK PEPPER

1 POUND SEA SCALLOPS

¾ POUND ASPARAGUS, CUT INTO
   2-INCH LENGTHS

1 LARGE RED BELL PEPPER, CUT INTO
   THIN STRIPS

2 TABLESPOONS REDUCED-SODIUM SOY
   SAUCE

¼ TEASPOON RED PEPPER FLAKES

1. In a medium saucepan, warm the vegetable oil over medium-high heat. Add the onion and cook until golden, about 4 minutes.

2. Stir in 2 tablespoons of the curry powder. Add the rice, 1 cup of water, 1 cup of the broth, the salt, and sugar, and bring to a boil. Reduce the heat to low, cover, and cook until the rice is tender, about 20 minutes.

3. Meanwhile, in a large skillet, warm 1 tablespoon of the sesame oil over medium-high heat. Add the garlic, scallions, and ginger, and stir-fry until the scallions are softened, about 3 minutes.

4. In a shallow bowl, combine the cornstarch and black pepper. Dredge the scallops in the cornstarch mixture. Add the remaining 1 tablespoon sesame oil and the scallops to the skillet, and stir-fry until the scallops begin to brown, about 4 minutes.

5. Add the asparagus, bell pepper, soy sauce, red pepper flakes, and the remaining ¼ cup broth and 1 tablespoon curry powder. Bring to a boil, stirring. Reduce the heat to low, cover, and simmer, stirring often, until the scallops are cooked through, about 7 minutes.

6. Serve the scallops over the curried rice.

Spicy Shrimp on Zucchini Nests

SERVES 4

2 LARGE UNPEELED ZUCCHINI,
  SHREDDED
2 LARGE UNPEELED YELLOW SQUASH,
  SHREDDED
1 TEASPOON SALT
1 POUND MEDIUM SHRIMP
2 TABLESPOONS OLIVE OIL
4 TABLESPOONS UNSALTED BUTTER

¼ TEASPOON BLACK PEPPER
3 CLOVES GARLIC, MINCED
⅓ CUP CHICKEN BROTH
2 TABLESPOONS FINE UNSEASONED DRY
  BREAD CRUMBS
½ TEASPOON RED PEPPER FLAKES
¼ CUP CHOPPED PARSLEY (OPTIONAL)

1. Layer the shredded zucchini and yellow squash in a colander, sprinkling it with the salt as you put it in. Set the colander in the sink to drain while you prepare the shrimp.

2. Shell and devein the shrimp.

3. Rinse the squash and drain well.

4. In a large skillet, warm 1 tablespoon of the oil with 2 tablespoons of the butter over medium-high heat until the butter is melted. Add the shredded squash and cook, stirring, until the vegetables are just limp, 2 to 3 minutes. Stir in the black pepper. Remove the squash to a bowl and cover loosely with foil to keep warm.

5. In the same skillet, warm the remaining 1 tablespoon oil with the remaining 2 tablespoons butter over medium-high heat until the butter is melted. Add the garlic and shrimp, and stir-fry until the shrimp are just beginning to turn pink, about 3 minutes.

6. Add the broth, bring to a boil, and cook, stirring, for 1 minute. Add the bread crumbs, red pepper flakes, and parsley (if using), and cook until the shrimp are cooked through, about 1 minute.

7. To serve, use a slotted spoon to transfer some of the squash to a dinner plate and top the squash "nest" with some of the shrimp.

LEMON-GARLIC
SHRIMP WITH PARSLIED RICE

SERVES 4

2 CUPS CHICKEN BROTH, PREFERABLY
  REDUCED-SODIUM
1 CUP RICE
2 TABLESPOONS OLIVE OIL
2 TABLESPOONS UNSALTED BUTTER
8 SCALLIONS, COARSELY CHOPPED
5 GARLIC CLOVES, MINCED
1 POUND LARGE SHRIMP, SHELLED AND
  DEVEINED

3 TABLESPOONS FRESH LEMON JUICE
¼ TEASPOON BLACK PEPPER
½ CUP GRATED PARMESAN CHEESE
2 TABLESPOONS CHOPPED PARSLEY
LEMON SLICES, FOR GARNISH
  (OPTIONAL)

1. In a medium saucepan, bring the broth to a boil over medium-high heat. Add the rice, reduce the heat to low, cover, and simmer until the rice is tender and the liquid is absorbed, about 20 minutes.

2. Meanwhile, in a large skillet, warm the oil with the butter over medium heat until the butter is melted. Add the scallions and garlic, and cook, stirring, until the scallions soften and begin to brown, about 3 minutes.

3. Add the shrimp and cook for 4 minutes. Stir in the lemon juice and pepper, and cook until the shrimp turn pink, about 4 minutes.

4. Stir the Parmesan and parsley into the cooked rice, then transfer the rice to a serving platter. Spoon the shrimp mixture on top of the rice and serve, garnished with lemon slices, if desired.

Variation: *Try this shrimp dish with lime juice (and sliced lime for garnish) in place of the lemon. Replace the parsley in the rice with chopped cilantro and increase the quantity to ¼ cup.*

SAUTÉED SHRIMP
WITH SHERRY AND CHILIES

SERVES 4

◇ LOW-FAT

1 POUND SHRIMP, SHELLED AND
DEVEINED, SHELLS RESERVED

1 WHOLE GARLIC BULB, CLOVES
SEPARATED AND PEELED

4 DRIED RED CHILI PEPPERS

1 TEASPOON FRESH ROSEMARY, OR
½ TEASPOON DRIED

½ TEASPOON FENNEL SEEDS

⅓ CUP DRY SHERRY

1 RED BELL PEPPER, CUT INTO
MATCHSTICKS

1 SCALLION, CUT INTO MATCHSTICKS

1 TABLESPOON UNSALTED BUTTER

1. In a medium saucepan, combine the shrimp shells with the garlic, chili peppers, rosemary, fennel seeds, and 1 quart of water. Bring to a boil, then reduce the heat to medium-low, and simmer the mixture for 30 minutes.

2. Strain the poaching liquid, discard the solids, and return the liquid to the saucepan. Boil the liquid rapidly until only about 1½ cups remain, 5 to 10 minutes.

3. Pour in the sherry and bring the liquid to a simmer. Add the shrimp and poach until they are opaque, about 1 minute. Remove the shrimp with a slotted spoon and set aside.

4. Boil the remaining poaching liquid until only 2 to 3 tablespoons remain, about 5 minutes. Add the bell pepper, reduce the heat to medium, and cook until softened, about 2 minutes.

5. Return the shrimp to the saucepan. Add the scallion and butter, and stir until the butter has melted and the shrimp are warm. Serve hot.

Garlic Shrimp with Cuban Black Bean Salad

SERVES 4

2 TABLESPOONS CHOPPED CHIVES OR
SCALLION GREENS

¼ CUP OLIVE OIL

¼ CUP FRESH LEMON JUICE

1½ TEASPOONS GRATED LEMON ZEST

½ TEASPOON SALT

¼ TEASPOON RED PEPPER FLAKES

¼ TEASPOON BLACK PEPPER

6 GARLIC CLOVES, MINCED

1 MEDIUM RED ONION, COARSELY
CHOPPED

1 LARGE GREEN BELL PEPPER, COARSELY
CHOPPED

1 MEDIUM RED BELL PEPPER, COARSELY
CHOPPED

2 CELERY RIBS, COARSELY CHOPPED

ONE 15-OUNCE CAN BLACK BEANS,
RINSED AND DRAINED

1 POUND MEDIUM SHRIMP, SHELLED
AND DEVEINED

1. In a food processor, combine the chives, 2 tablespoons of the olive oil, the lemon juice, lemon zest, salt, red pepper flakes, and black pepper. Process the dressing to blend.

2. In a large skillet, warm 1 tablespoon of the olive oil over medium-high heat. Add 1 teaspoon of the minced garlic, the onion, bell peppers, and celery, and stir-fry until the vegetables are crisp-tender, 3 to 4 minutes.

3. Stir the black beans into the skillet and cook until heated through, about 1 minute. Transfer the vegetables and beans to a serving bowl or platter. Pour the dressing over the mixture and toss to thoroughly combine; set aside.

4. Add the remaining 1 tablespoon olive oil to the skillet and warm over medium-high heat. Add the remaining garlic and stir-fry until it begins to brown, about 2 minutes. Add the shrimp and cook until the shrimp turn pink and are opaque throughout, about 4 minutes.

5. Serve the shrimp on a bed of black bean salad.

BAKED TARRAGON FISH

SERVES 4

1 SMALL RED ONION, FINELY CHOPPED

2 GARLIC CLOVES, MINCED

½ CUP WHITE WINE VINEGAR OR CIDER
   VINEGAR

1 TEASPOON TARRAGON

¼ TEASPOON SUGAR

¼ TEASPOON SALT

¼ TEASPOON BLACK PEPPER

8 LARGE NAPA CABBAGE LEAVES

1 POUND SOLE OR FLOUNDER FILLETS

4 TEASPOONS UNSALTED BUTTER

4 BAY LEAVES

1. Preheat the oven to 375°. Line a baking sheet or broiler pan with foil. Lightly grease the foil.

2. In a small saucepan, combine the onion, garlic, vinegar, tarragon, sugar, salt, and pepper, and bring to a boil over medium-high heat. Reduce the heat to low, cover, and simmer for 10 minutes.

3. Meanwhile, place 4 of the cabbage leaves on the prepared broiler pan. Cut the fish into 4 equal portions and place one on each leaf.

Dividing evenly, spoon the vinegar mixture over each fish. Dot each fish with 1 teaspoon of the butter and top with a bay leaf. Cover the fish with the second cabbage leaf.

4. Bake the fish for 5 to 8 minutes, or until the fish just flakes when tested with a fork.

SUBSTITUTION: *If you can't get napa cabbage (a crisp, crinkly Chinese cabbage), cook the fish in large leaves of Savoy cabbage, Romaine lettuce, or Swiss chard.*

Codfish Cakes with Horseradish Sauce

SERVES 4

¾ POUND COD FILLETS, FINELY
  CHOPPED

1¼ CUPS FINE UNSEASONED DRY BREAD
  CRUMBS

1 WHOLE EGG

1 EGG WHITE

¾ CUP FINELY CHOPPED ONION

¼ CUP CHOPPED PARSLEY

3 GARLIC CLOVES, MINCED

2 TABLESPOONS GRAINY MUSTARD

2 TABLESPOONS ANISETTE OR OTHER
  ANISE-FLAVORED LIQUEUR
  (OPTIONAL)

2 TABLESPOONS FRESH LEMON JUICE

1½ TEASPOONS CAPERS, CHOPPED

1 TABLESPOON PAPRIKA

¼ TEASPOON CAYENNE PEPPER

⅔ CUP PLAIN LOW-FAT YOGURT

2 TABLESPOONS RED WINE VINEGAR

1 TEASPOON HORSERADISH

1. Preheat the oven to 400°. Lightly oil a large baking sheet.

2. In a large mixing bowl, combine the fish, ½ cup of the bread crumbs, the whole egg, egg white, onion, all but 1 tablespoon of the parsley, the garlic, 1 tablespoon of the mustard, the anisette (if using), lemon juice, capers, paprika, and cayenne, and toss to mix thoroughly.

3. Place the remaining ¾ cup bread crumbs in a shallow bowl. Divide the fish mixture into 8 equal portions. Pat each portion into a cake about ¾ inch thick. Coat the cakes well with the bread crumbs and place them on the prepared baking sheet. Bake the codfish cakes for 20 minutes.

4. Meanwhile, combine the yogurt, vinegar, horseradish, and the remaining 1 tablespoon each mustard and parsley.

5. Serve the cakes with a dollop of sauce on the side.

Flounder Rolls
Stuffed with Cheese and Spinach

SERVES 4

◇ LOW - FAT

HALF OF A 10-OUNCE PACKAGE
   FROZEN CHOPPED SPINACH, THAWED
   AND SQUEEZED DRY
3 GARLIC CLOVES, MINCED
1 SMALL ONION, FINELY CHOPPED
½ CUP COTTAGE CHEESE
½ CUP CRUMBLED FETA CHEESE OR
   2 OUNCES NEUFCHÂTEL CREAM
   CHEESE, CUT INTO SMALL PIECES

1 EGG
2 TEASPOONS GRATED LEMON ZEST
3 TABLESPOONS FLOUR
1 TEASPOON OREGANO
¼ TEASPOON BLACK PEPPER
4 FLOUNDER OR SOLE FILLETS (ABOUT
   1 POUND TOTAL)
¼ CUP FRESH LEMON JUICE
4 TEASPOONS UNSALTED BUTTER

1. Preheat the oven to 350°. Butter an 11 x 7-inch baking dish.

2. In a medium bowl, combine the spinach, garlic, onion, cottage cheese, feta, egg, lemon zest, flour, oregano, and pepper.

3. Place the fillets on a work surface. Dividing evenly, spread each fillet with the filling. Loosely roll up the fillets and place them seam-side down in the prepared baking dish.

4. Pour the lemon juice over the fish and dot each roll with 1 teaspoon of the butter. Bake the fish for 20 minutes, or until the fish just flakes when tested with a fork. About halfway through the baking time, spoon some of the melted butter and lemon juice over the fish.

BAKED COD WITH
TOMATOES AND PROVOLONE

SERVES 4

1 TABLESPOON OLIVE OIL

¼ TEASPOON BLACK PEPPER

¼ TEASPOON SALT

1 POUND COD FILLETS

2 TABLESPOONS CHOPPED FRESH BASIL,
OR 1 TABLESPOON DRIED

2 GARLIC CLOVES, MINCED

ONE 14-OUNCE CAN NO-SALT-ADDED
WHOLE TOMATOES, DRAINED AND
CHOPPED

1 SMALL ZUCCHINI, THINLY SLICED ON
THE DIAGONAL

2 OUNCES PROVOLONE CHEESE, CUT
INTO THIN STRIPS

1. Preheat the oven to 400°. Spread the oil in the bottom of a casserole.

2. Sprinkle the pepper and ⅛ teaspoon of the salt over both sides of the fillets. Arrange the fillets in the casserole in a single layer.

3. Sprinkle the basil and garlic over the fish, then cover the fish with the tomatoes. Arrange the zucchini slices in a fish-scale pattern down the center of the dish; sprinkle the remaining ⅛ teaspoon of salt over them.

4. Cover the dish with foil and bake for 10 minutes. Remove the foil and place the strips of provolone in a crisscross pattern over the zucchini. Cover the dish again and bake until the fish feels firm to the touch, 3 to 5 minutes. Serve hot.

KITCHEN NOTE: *Provolone is a pale straw-colored cheese with a delicately smoky flavor. It's made by the same process as mozzarella, and has a similar (though firmer) texture. Like mozzarella, provolone melts beautifully. Keep it on hand to use in grilled sandwiches, omelets, and baked pasta dishes.*

FILLETS OF FLOUNDER SORRENTO

SERVES 4

3 TABLESPOONS OLIVE OIL

1 LARGE ONION, THINLY SLICED

2 TEASPOONS MINCED GARLIC

1 CUP CHOPPED NO-SALT-ADDED
   CANNED TOMATOES

1 TABLESPOON CHOPPED FRESH
   OREGANO, OR 1 TEASPOON DRIED

½ TEASPOON BLACK PEPPER

¼ CUP PITTED BLACK OLIVES,
   COARSELY CHOPPED

2 TABLESPOONS CAPERS

4 FLOUNDER FILLETS (ABOUT 1½
   POUNDS TOTAL)

½ CUP DRY WHITE WINE

1. In a medium skillet, warm the oil over medium heat. Add the onion and sauté, stirring occasionally, until light golden, about 8 minutes.

2. Add the garlic and sauté for 1 minute. Add the tomatoes, oregano, and pepper. Reduce the heat to medium-low and simmer until the sauce is thickened, about 15 minutes.

3. Meanwhile, preheat the oven to 450°.

4. Add the olives and capers to the sauce, and simmer for 5 minutes to blend the flavors. Remove the pan from the heat.

5. Coat the baking dish with a spoonful of the sauce. Place a fillet in the dish and top with a spoonful of the sauce. Overlap with a second fillet and top with sauce. Add the remaining fish and sauce in the same manner.

6. Pour the wine over the fish and bake for 6 to 8 minutes, or until the fish just flakes when tested with a fork.

7. Transfer the fish to a platter. Strain the pan juices into a small saucepan. Cook over high heat until slightly thickened, 2 to 3 minutes. Pour the reduced pan juices over the fillets and serve.

Shrimp-Stuffed Baked Fish

SERVES 4

1 TABLESPOON UNSALTED BUTTER

1 GARLIC CLOVE, MINCED

1 SMALL ONION, COARSELY CHOPPED

1 MEDIUM CARROT, FINELY CHOPPED

1 CELERY RIB, FINELY CHOPPED

1½ TEASPOONS THYME

¼ POUND COOKED BABY SHRIMP

4 SOLE OR FLOUNDER FILLETS (ABOUT
    1½ POUNDS TOTAL)

⅔ CUP BOTTLED CLAM JUICE OR
    REDUCED-SODIUM CHICKEN BROTH

1 TABLESPOON CORNSTARCH

¼ CUP HEAVY CREAM

¼ TEASPOON SALT

¼ TEASPOON BLACK PEPPER

1. Preheat the oven to 375°. Lightly grease a baking dish large enough to hold four rolled fillets in one layer (about 8 x 8).

2. In a medium skillet, warm the butter over medium-high heat until it is melted. Add the garlic and onion, and sauté until the onion begins to soften, about 3 minutes. Add the carrot, celery, and 1 teaspoon of the thyme. Cook until the vegetables begin to soften, about 4 minutes. Remove from the heat and stir in the shrimp.

3. Place 3 tablespoons of the stuffing on each fillet and loosely roll up. Place the rolls and any leftover stuffing in the prepared baking dish and pour in the clam juice. Cover with foil and bake for 20 minutes, or until the fish just flakes when tested with a fork.

4. Meanwhile, in a small bowl, blend the cornstarch, heavy cream, salt, pepper, and the remaining ½ teaspoon thyme.

5. Transfer the fish rolls to a plate and cover loosely with foil to keep warm. Transfer the cooking juices and the extra stuffing to a saucepan. Bring the mixture to a boil over medium-high heat. Add the cornstarch mixture and cook, stirring, until thickened slightly, about 3 minutes. Serve the fish rolls topped with the sauce.

GREEK-STYLE BAKED HADDOCK

SERVES 4

◇ LOW-FAT

1 POUND HADDOCK FILLETS

2 LARGE TOMATOES, SLICED

2 SMALL ONIONS, SLICED

1 SMALL FENNEL BULB, SLICED
   CROSSWISE

2 GARLIC CLOVES, MINCED

1 TABLESPOON CHOPPED FRESH
   OREGANO, OR 2 TEASPOONS DRIED

3 TABLESPOONS DRY WHITE WINE

½ CUP CRUMBLED FETA CHEESE

2 TABLESPOONS CHOPPED PARSLEY

4 PITTED BLACK OLIVES, SLICED

½ TEASPOON BLACK PEPPER

1. Preheat the oven to 375°. Lightly oil a large baking dish.

2. Cut the fish crosswise into 2-inch-wide strips.

3. Layer the tomatoes, onions, fennel, garlic, and oregano in the bottom of the prepared baking dish. Arrange the fish on top of the vegetables and sprinkle it with the wine.

4. Cover the dish with foil and bake for 15 to 20 minutes, or until the fish is opaque and feels firm to the touch.

5. Remove the dish from the oven. Sprinkle the fish with the feta, parsley, olives, and pepper. Serve hot, spooning the pan juices over each portion.

Substitution: *When fennel is not available (it's an autumn vegetable and you may not find it in your market year-round), substitute 2 cups of sliced celery and 1 teaspoon of fennel seeds. If you have a mortar and pestle, crush the fennel seeds first to release the flavors. Add the fennel seeds and sliced celery in Step 3.*

SKILLET-BAKED
FLOUNDER PROVENÇALE

SERVES 4

2 TABLESPOONS OLIVE OIL

1 MEDIUM ONION, COARSELY CHOPPED

3 GARLIC CLOVES, MINCED

1½ CUPS NO-SALT-ADDED CANNED
   TOMATO SAUCE

¼ CUP DRY RED WINE OR CHICKEN
   BROTH

¾ TEASPOON TARRAGON

¼ TEASPOON BLACK PEPPER

¾ CUP PITTED BLACK OLIVES

¼ CUP CHOPPED PARSLEY (OPTIONAL)

4 SMALL FLOUNDER FILLETS (ABOUT
   1½ POUNDS TOTAL)

2 TABLESPOONS FINE UNSEASONED DRY
   BREAD CRUMBS

1. In a large ovenproof skillet (preferably not cast iron), warm 1 tablespoon of the oil over medium-high heat. Add the onion and garlic, and cook, stirring occasionally, until the mixture begins to brown, about 5 minutes.

2. Add the tomato sauce, red wine, tarragon, and pepper, and bring the mixture to a boil. Reduce the heat to low, cover, and simmer for 15 minutes.

3. Meanwhile, preheat the oven to 375°.

4. Add the olives and 2 tablespoons of the parsley (if using) to the skillet. Add the flounder and spoon some of the sauce on top.

5. Sprinkle the fish with the bread crumbs and drizzle with the remaining 1 tablespoon oil. Place the skillet in the oven and bake, uncovered, for 10 minutes, or until the fish just flakes when tested with a fork.

6. Serve hot, garnished with the remaining parsley, if desired.

Mushroom-Smothered Baked Fish

SERVES 4

1 TABLESPOON OLIVE OIL

2 TABLESPOONS UNSALTED BUTTER

1 LARGE CARROT, FINELY CHOPPED

1 CELERY RIB, COARSELY CHOPPED

¼ POUND MUSHROOMS, COARSELY
  CHOPPED

1 SLICE FIRM-TEXTURED BREAD,
  COARSELY CHOPPED

1½ TEASPOONS OREGANO

½ TEASPOON SALT

¼ TEASPOON BLACK PEPPER

3 TABLESPOONS SOUR CREAM

3 TABLESPOONS PLAIN LOW-FAT
  YOGURT

4 RED SNAPPER, GROUPER, OR OCEAN
  PERCH FILLETS (ABOUT 1½ POUNDS
  TOTAL)

2 TABLESPOONS GRATED PARMESAN
  CHEESE

1. Preheat the oven to 400°. Line a broiler pan with foil and lightly grease the foil.

2. In a medium skillet, warm the oil with the butter over medium-high heat until the butter is melted. Add the carrot, celery, and mushrooms, and stir-fry until the vegetables begin to soften, 3 to 4 minutes.

3. Remove the skillet from the heat and stir in the bread crumbs, oregano, salt, and pepper. In a small bowl, blend the sour cream and yogurt.

4. Place the fish on the broiler pan. Coat the fish with the sour cream-yogurt mixture, then spread evenly with the bread crumb mixture. Sprinkle with the Parmesan.

5. Bake the fish for 15 to 18 minutes, or until it just flakes when tested with a fork.

Buttermilk Baked Halibut

SERVES 4

1 CUP BUTTERMILK

¼ TEASPOON SALT

½ TEASPOON BLACK PEPPER

4 HALIBUT STEAKS (1½ POUNDS
TOTAL)

1 CUP FRESH BREAD CRUMBS

½ CUP REDUCED-FAT MAYONNAISE

½ CUP PLAIN LOW-FAT YOGURT

2 TABLESPOONS DRY WHITE WINE

¼ CUP CHOPPED ONION

PAPRIKA, FOR DUSTING

1 LEMON, CUT INTO 4 WEDGES

1. In a shallow dish large enough to hold the fish snugly in one layer, combine the buttermilk, salt, and pepper. Add the fish and marinate for 30 minutes at room temperature.

2. Preheat the oven to 500°. Lightly grease a shallow baking dish.

3. Place the bread crumbs in a shallow bowl. Drain the halibut thoroughly on paper towels and then dip both sides of the steaks in the bread crumbs, reserving the excess. Arrange the fish in the prepared baking dish.

4. In a small bowl, blend the mayonnaise, yogurt, wine, and onion. With a spatula, carefully spread the mayonnaise mixture evenly over the fish. Cover evenly with the remaining bread crumbs and dust with paprika. Bake for 10 minutes, or until the fish just flakes when tested with a fork.

5. Serve with the lemon wedges.

Substitution: *If you don't have buttermilk on hand, you can make a reasonable approximation of it by stirring 1 tablespoon of vinegar or lemon juice into 1 cup of room-temperature milk. Let the milk stand for about 5 minutes before using.*

SOLE BAKED IN PARCHMENT

SERVES 4

4 SMALL SOLE OR FLOUNDER FILLETS
(ABOUT 1 POUND TOTAL)
1 SMALL ZUCCHINI, THINLY SLICED
1 SMALL YELLOW SQUASH, THINLY
SLICED
3 LARGE MUSHROOMS, THINLY SLICED
4 FRESH THYME SPRIGS, OR
1 TEASPOON DRIED THYME

¼ CUP DRY VERMOUTH OR DRY WHITE
WINE
2 TABLESPOONS UNSALTED BUTTER,
CUT INTO SMALL PIECES
¼ TEASPOON SALT
½ TEASPOON BLACK PEPPER

1. Preheat the oven to 425°. Using a diagonal lengthwise cut, divide each fillet in half to make one thick fillet and one thin one.

2. Cut out four 12 x 18-inch pieces of parchment paper or foil. Lightly butter each piece.

3. In the center of each piece of parchment or foil, layer the fish and vegetables: Begin with a bed of zucchini and yellow squash (but save enough of both to form a top layer). Place a thick fillet on the squash bed and top the fillet with the mushrooms. Put a thin fillet on top of the mushrooms, and top it with a final layer of squash. To each layered assem-

bly, add a sprig of fresh thyme (or ¼ teaspoon dried), 1 tablespoon of the vermouth, 1½ teaspoons of the butter, a pinch of salt, and ⅛ teaspoon of the pepper.

4. Bring the two short sides of the parchment or foil together and fold over as you would to wrap a sandwich. Fold in the ends to seal the packets. Transfer the packages to a baking sheet. Bake them for 10 minutes per inch of thickness of the entire assembly, about 15 minutes.

5. Put the packages on individual plates. Let each diner open his own package.

Fillets of Sole in Wine Sauce

SERVES 4

1 CUP CHOPPED ONION

½ CUP CHOPPED CARROT

1 TABLESPOON CHOPPED FRESH THYME,
   OR 1 TEASPOON DRIED

1 TABLESPOON MINCED FRESH DILL, OR
   1 TEASPOON DRIED

1 TEASPOON CRUSHED FENNEL SEEDS
   (OPTIONAL)

1 BAY LEAF

4 SOLE OR FLOUNDER FILLETS (½ INCH
   THICK, ABOUT 1¾ POUNDS TOTAL)

½ CUP DRY WHITE WINE

¼ TEASPOON SALT

¼ TEASPOON BLACK PEPPER

2 TABLESPOONS UNSALTED BUTTER

2 TABLESPOONS FLOUR

1. Preheat the oven to 375°. Cut a sheet of wax paper to fit into an 11 x 7-inch baking dish and butter lightly.

2. Place the onion, carrot, thyme, dill, fennel seeds, and bay leaf in the prepared baking dish. Top with the fillets. Add the wine, ½ cup of water, the salt, and pepper. Cover with the wax paper, buttered-side down. Top with a sheet of foil and crimp the foil around the edges of the dish.

3. Bake for 12 to 15 minutes, or until the fish just flakes when tested with a fork.

4. Meanwhile, in a small bowl, blend the butter with the flour.

5. Remove the fish from the oven and transfer to dinner plates. Drain the pan juices through a sieve set over a small saucepan. Over low heat, add the butter-flour mixture a bit at a time and whisk until blended and thickened, 2 to 3 minutes. Spoon the sauce over the fish.

Baked Sole with Mushrooms and Tomatoes

SERVES 4

2 TABLESPOONS PLUS 1 TEASPOON
    OLIVE OIL
1 TABLESPOON UNSALTED BUTTER
½ POUND MUSHROOMS, THINLY SLICED
4 SOLE, FLOUNDER, OR RED SNAPPER
    FILLETS (ABOUT 1½ POUNDS TOTAL)
3 TABLESPOONS FRESH LEMON JUICE

¼ TEASPOON SALT
¼ TEASPOON BLACK PEPPER
1½ CUPS CHOPPED SCALLIONS
2 TABLESPOONS CHOPPED PARSLEY
3 CUPS CUBED TOMATOES (ABOUT 4
    MEDIUM)

1. Preheat the oven to 500°.

2. In a medium nonstick skillet, warm 1 tablespoon of the oil with the butter. Add the mushrooms and cook until they exude their liquid, about 5 minutes.

3. Arrange the fish fillets in a single layer in a baking dish. Sprinkle the fish with the lemon juice and ⅛ teaspoon each of the salt and pepper. Sprinkle with 2 teaspoons of the oil.

Spread each fillet with the mushrooms. Top with the scallions, parsley, and tomatoes. Sprinkle with the remaining 2 teaspoons oil and ⅛ teaspoon each salt and pepper.

4. Place the fish in the oven and bake for about 6 minutes, or until the fish just flakes when tested with a fork.

VARIATION: *Try flavorful shiitakes in place of button mushrooms. Trim and discard the stems; add a little more oil (or some chicken stock) to the pan if the shiitakes seem to be drying out.*

BAKED SOLE WITH ZUCCHINI AND PEPPERS

SERVES 4

4 SMALL ZUCCHINI

1 TEASPOON SALT

2 RED BELL PEPPERS, CUT INTO 3 OR 4 FLAT PANELS, CORES AND SEEDS DISCARDED

1½ POUNDS SOLE OR FLOUNDER FILLETS

1 TABLESPOON PLUS 1 TEASPOON GRAINY MUSTARD

3 TABLESPOONS UNSALTED BUTTER

2 SHALLOTS, COARSELY CHOPPED

¼ TEASPOON BLACK PEPPER

DASH OF NUTMEG

1. Grate the zucchini in a food processor or with the large holes of a hand-held grater. Place the zucchini in a colander, toss with the salt, and set over a plate to drain for at least 15 minutes.

2. Meanwhile, preheat the broiler. Place the pepper pieces, skin-side up, on a baking sheet and broil as close to the heat as possible for 10 minutes, or until evenly charred. Transfer the pepper pieces to a bowl and cover with a plate for about 5 minutes to steam the peppers. Turn the oven down to 425°.

3. Flatten the fish fillets so they are of even thickness, about ¼ inch thick. Cut into serving pieces. Spread the fish with mustard on both sides and arrange in a single layer in a buttered baking dish. Set aside while you prepare the vegetables.

4. Peel the skin off the roasted pepper pieces and cut them into thin strips. By handfuls, thoroughly squeeze all the excess liquid from the zucchini.

5. In a medium skillet, warm the butter over medium heat until melted. Add the shallots and sauté until translucent, about 1 minute. Add the zucchini and sauté for 2 minutes. Season with the black pepper and nutmeg. Add the roasted pepper strips and cook until heated through, 2 to 3 minutes. Set aside to keep warm.

6. Bake the fillets for 4 to 6 minutes, or until they just flake when tested with a fork. Transfer the fish to dinner plates and serve with the vegetables on the side.

FOIL-BAKED SOLE AND VEGETABLES WITH HERB BUTTER

SERVES 4

4 SOLE FILLETS (ABOUT 1½ POUNDS TOTAL)

4 SCALLIONS, COARSELY CHOPPED

1 LARGE CARROT, THINLY SLICED

1 CELERY RIB, THINLY SLICED

⅓ CUP UNSALTED BUTTER, AT ROOM TEMPERATURE

3 TABLESPOONS CHOPPED PARSLEY

1 GARLIC CLOVE, MINCED

½ TEASPOON TARRAGON

¼ TEASPOON SALT

¼ TEASPOON BLACK PEPPER

1. Preheat the oven to 425°. Cut out four 12-inch squares of foil.

2. Place one fish fillet in the center of each sheet of foil. Dividing evenly, sprinkle the scallions, carrot, and celery on top of the fish.

3. In a small bowl, beat together the butter, parsley, garlic, tarragon, salt, and pepper. Divide the herb butter evenly among the 4 packets.

4. Bring two sides of foil together and fold over as you would to wrap a sandwich. Fold in the ends to seal the packets. Place the foil packets on a baking sheet and bake for 12 minutes, or until the fish is opaque throughout and just flakes when tested with a fork.

5. Transfer the fish and vegetables to individual dinner plates, being sure to pour any butter and juices from the packet on top of the fish.

BOURBON-BASTED SALMON

SERVES 4

◆ EXTRA-QUICK

½ CUP BOURBON

½ CUP OLIVE OIL

3 TABLESPOONS REDUCED-SODIUM SOY
SAUCE

4 SALMON FILLETS OR STEAKS (¾ TO
1 INCH THICK, ABOUT 2 POUNDS
TOTAL)

1. Preheat the oven to 450°. Line a baking pan with foil.

2. In a small bowl, combine the bourbon, oil, and soy sauce, and whisk until blended.

3. Place the salmon skin-side down in the baking pan and brush with some of the basting mixture. Bake, uncovered, basting 2 or 3 times, for 15 to 20 minutes, or until the fish just flakes when tested with a fork.

4. In a small saucepan, bring the remaining basting mixture to a boil over medium-high heat. Reduce the heat and simmer for 3 to 4 minutes.

5. Transfer the salmon fillets to dinner plates and serve the basting mixture on the side.

SWEET AFTERTHOUGHT: *An elegant dessert for this equally elegant dish is made by halving large lemons lengthwise and scooping out the pulp (save it for making lemonade). Pack softened lemon or orange sorbet into the lemon shells, smooth the surface, and cover with plastic wrap. Freeze the sorbet-filled shells until serving time. To serve, garnish with mint sprigs or fresh raspberries.*

HERB-COATED SALMON

SERVES 4

◆ EXTRA-QUICK

2 GARLIC CLOVES

¼ CUP (PACKED) PARSLEY SPRIGS

4 SCALLIONS

1 TABLESPOON OLIVE OIL

2 TEASPOONS GRATED LEMON ZEST

1 TEASPOON TARRAGON

½ TEASPOON SALT

¼ TEASPOON BLACK PEPPER

4 SALMON FILLETS (¾ TO 1 INCH
    THICK, ABOUT 1 POUND TOTAL)

2 TABLESPOONS FRESH LEMON JUICE

1. Preheat the oven to 425°. Line a baking sheet with foil and lightly grease the foil.

2. In a food processor, finely chop the garlic. Add the parsley and finely chop. Add the scallions and pulse briefly until they are just chopped. Transfer the mixture to a bowl and stir in the oil, lemon zest, tarragon, salt, and pepper.

3. Place the salmon skin-side down on the prepared baking sheet. Coat the fish with the herb mixture. Bake for about 15 minutes, or until the salmon just flakes when tested with a fork.

4. Sprinkle the fish with the lemon juice before serving.

VARIATION: *For the fresh parsley and the dried tarragon called for in this recipe, substitute a total of ½ cup fresh dill. Add it all to the food processor when you chop the garlic and scallions.*

BAKED RED SNAPPER WITH CHILI SAUCE

SERVES 4

¼ CUP COARSELY CHOPPED ORANGE
ZEST

1 TABLESPOON COARSELY CHOPPED
LEMON ZEST

2 TEASPOONS COARSELY CHOPPED LIME
ZEST

1½ CUPS FRESH ORANGE JUICE

2 TABLESPOONS FRESH LEMON JUICE

3 TABLESPOONS FRESH LIME JUICE

⅓ CUP OLIVE OIL

1 TABLESPOON CIDER VINEGAR

1 LARGE GARLIC CLOVE, PEELED

½ CUP MILD CHILI POWDER

1 TEASPOON SALT

½ TEASPOON BLACK PEPPER

DASH OF CAYENNE PEPPER

4 RED SNAPPER, OCEAN PERCH, OR SEA
BASS FILLETS (¾ INCH THICK,
ABOUT 2 POUNDS TOTAL)

1. Preheat the oven to 450°. Cut out four 12 x 16-inch pieces of parchment paper or foil.

2. Place the orange, lemon, and lime zests in a food processor or blender. Gradually add the orange juice, lemon juice, lime juice, oil, vinegar, garlic, chili powder, salt, black pepper, and cayenne, and process until smooth.

3. Place one fillet in the center of each piece of parchment or foil. Spoon 2 tablespoons of the sauce over each fillet and scrape the remaining sauce into a small saucepan.

4. Bring the two short sides of the parchment or foil together and fold over as you would to wrap a sandwich. Fold in the ends to seal the packets. Place the fish packets in the baking dish and bake for 8 minutes.

5. Meanwhile, bring the remaining sauce to a simmer over medium-high heat, stirring frequently. Reduce the heat to low and cook the sauce, uncovered, until the fish is ready.

6. Remove the fish from the oven and open the packets. Transfer the fish to dinner plates and top with sauce.

SKILLET-BAKED TROUT
WITH LEMON-CAPER SAUCE

SERVES 4

3 SLICES OF BACON

½ CUP FLOUR

½ CUP CORNMEAL

¼ TEASPOON SALT

½ TEASPOON BLACK PEPPER

4 SMALL WHOLE BROOK TROUT (ABOUT
½ POUND EACH)

2 TABLESPOONS OLIVE OIL

2 TABLESPOONS UNSALTED BUTTER

3 TABLESPOONS FRESH LEMON JUICE

2 TABLESPOONS CAPERS

2 TEASPOONS GRATED LEMON ZEST

¼ CUP CHOPPED PARSLEY (OPTIONAL)

1. Preheat the oven to 425°.

2. In a large ovenproof skillet, cook the bacon over medium heat until crisp, about 10 minutes. Drain the bacon on paper towels and set aside. Pour off all but 1 tablespoon of bacon fat from the skillet.

3. Meanwhile, in a shallow dish or pie plate, combine the flour, cornmeal, salt, and pepper. Dredge the whole trout in the seasoned flour-cornmeal mixture.

4. Add 1 tablespoon of the oil to the bacon fat in the skillet and warm over medium-high heat. Add the fish and cook until browned on both sides, about 2 minutes per side. Add the remaining 1 tablespoon oil as necessary to prevent sticking.

5. Place the skillet in the oven and bake for 15 minutes, or until the fish just flakes when tested with a fork. Remove the trout to individual dinner plates.

6. Return the skillet to the stovetop. Over medium-high heat, add the butter, lemon juice, capers, lemon zest, and parsley (if using). Cook, stirring, until heated through, about 1 minute.

7. Pour the lemon-caper sauce over the fish and crumble the bacon on top.

STRIPED BASS WITH FENNEL AND ROMAINE

SERVES 4

10 FENNEL STALKS, HALVED CROSSWISE

4 STRIPED BASS FILLETS (½ INCH THICK, ABOUT 2 POUNDS TOTAL)

2 GARLIC CLOVES, MINCED

⅓ CUP DRY WHITE WINE

4 TABLESPOONS UNSALTED BUTTER

¼ CUP OLIVE OIL

8 ROMAINE LETTUCE LEAVES

1. In a large skillet, bring ½ inch of water to a boil. Add the fennel, cover, and simmer until crisp-tender, about 10 minutes. Drain and set aside.

2. Meanwhile, preheat the oven to 350°. Generously butter a shallow baking dish.

3. Place the fish in the prepared baking dish and sprinkle with the minced garlic. Pour the wine over the fish and dot each fillet with 1 tablespoon butter. Top each with 5 pieces of fennel. Brush with 2 tablespoons of the oil.

Bake the fish until firm but still undercooked, 5 to 10 minutes, depending on the thickness of the fillets.

4. Drape the Romaine leaves loosely over the fish, and brush with the remaining 2 tablespoons oil. Bake for 5 minutes, or until the fish is still firm but just flakes when tested with a fork.

5. Divide the fillets among dinner plates and serve hot.

KITCHEN NOTE: *You need just the fennel stalks for this recipe, so plan to use the fennel bulb in another menu: Slivers of fennel make delicious, crunchy crudités to serve with salsa or creamy dips.*

Tuna Baked in Parchment with Red Peppers

SERVES 4

¼ CUP OLIVE OIL

4 RED BELL PEPPERS, SLIVERED

4 GARLIC CLOVES, MINCED

1 TEASPOON OREGANO

½ TEASPOON SALT

½ TEASPOON BLACK PEPPER

4 TUNA OR BLUEFISH FILLETS (1 INCH
   THICK, ABOUT 2 POUNDS TOTAL)

1 MEDIUM RED ONION, HALVED AND
   THINLY SLICED

1 FRESH JALAPEÑO PEPPER, SEEDED
   AND MINCED (OPTIONAL)

2 TABLESPOONS UNSALTED BUTTER

1. In a medium skillet, warm the oil over high heat. Add the bell peppers, reduce the heat to medium, and sauté, stirring, until tender, about 8 minutes. Add the garlic, oregano, and ¼ teaspoon each of the salt and pepper, and cook, stirring, for 30 seconds. Remove the pan from the heat and set aside.

2. Preheat the oven to 450°. Cut four 12 x 16-inch pieces of parchment paper or foil.

3. Place 1 fillet in the center of each piece. Season the fillets with the remaining ¼ teaspoon each salt and pepper, and top with the onion, bell pepper mixture, and jalapeño (if using). Dot each fillet with 1½ teaspoons of the butter.

4. Bring the two short sides of the parchment or foil together and fold over as you would to wrap a sandwich. Fold in the ends to seal the packets. Place the packets on a baking sheet and bake for 8 minutes.

5. Remove the fish from the oven. Slit the packets open and slide the fish and juices out onto dinner plates.

BAKED STUFFED SHRIMP WITH TOMATO TARTAR SAUCE

SERVES 4

1 SLICE OF BREAD

4 SCALLIONS

¼ CUP (PACKED) PARSLEY SPRIGS

1 GARLIC CLOVE

¼ CUP GRATED PARMESAN CHEESE

½ TEASPOON BLACK PEPPER

1 POUND LARGE OR MEDIUM SHRIMP

2 TABLESPOONS UNSALTED BUTTER, MELTED

1 MEDIUM PLUM TOMATO, FINELY CHOPPED

¼ CUP MAYONNAISE

¼ CUP PLAIN LOW-FAT YOGURT

1 TEASPOON FRESH LEMON JUICE

1 TEASPOON DRY MUSTARD

1 TEASPOON DIJON MUSTARD

¼ TEASPOON SALT

1. Preheat the oven to 425°. Line a baking sheet with foil.

2. In a food processor, combine the bread, 2 of the scallions, the parsley, and garlic, and pulse on and off to form coarse crumbs. Add the Parmesan and ¼ teaspoon of the pepper, and pulse just until mixed; set aside.

3. Shell the shrimp, leaving the tails on if desired. Devein the shrimp, cutting them as deeply as possible without actually cutting through them; spread the two sides of the shrimp apart to butterfly them slightly.

4. Place the shrimp, butterflied-side up, on the foil-lined baking sheet and flatten them

out. Place a heaping tablespoon of the stuffing on each shrimp, mounding it slightly, then drizzle the shrimp with the butter.

5. Bake the shrimp for about 11 minutes, or just until firm.

6. Meanwhile, finely chop the remaining 2 scallions. Combine them in a small bowl with the tomato, mayonnaise, yogurt, lemon juice, dry and Dijon mustards, salt, and remaining ¼ teaspoon pepper, and stir well.

7. Serve the shrimp with the tomato tartar sauce.

FLOUNDER WITH LEMON CREAM

SERVES 4

◆ EXTRA-QUICK

2 TABLESPOONS UNSALTED BUTTER,
    MELTED
¼ CUP FRESH LEMON JUICE
1 TABLESPOON GRATED LEMON ZEST
1 TEASPOON TARRAGON
½ TEASPOON SALT
½ TEASPOON BLACK PEPPER

4 SMALL FLOUNDER, SOLE, OR RED
    SNAPPER FILLETS (ABOUT 1¼
    POUNDS TOTAL)
1 TEASPOON DIJON MUSTARD
½ TEASPOON DRY MUSTARD
½ CUP HEAVY CREAM

1. Preheat the broiler. Line a broiler pan with foil.

2. In a small bowl, combine the melted butter, 2 tablespoons of the lemon juice, 1 teaspoon of the lemon zest, ½ teaspoon of the tarragon, the salt, and pepper.

3. Place the fish on the prepared broiler pan. Brush the lemon-butter mixture over the fish. Broil the fish 4 inches from the heat for about 7 minutes, or until the fish is cooked through and just flakes when tested with a fork.

4. Meanwhile, in a mixer bowl, combine the Dijon mustard, dry mustard, and the remaining 2 tablespoons lemon juice, 2 teaspoons lemon zest, and ½ teaspoon tarragon.

5. Gradually beat the cream into the mixture in a thin stream. Continue beating until the cream forms soft peaks. Be careful not to overbeat, as the lemon juice makes the cream more susceptible to curdling.

6. Serve the fish topped with a dollop of the lemon cream.

KITCHEN NOTE: *Although as rich and luxurious as a classic hollandaise or mousseline sauce, the lemon cream for this broiled flounder dish is much easier to make. One caution, however: Be careful not to overbeat the mixture as you add the cream. Keep your electric mixer on low speed, and don't hurry the process or the cream will "break." It's also best to start with well-chilled cream.*

LIME-DRESSED SNAPPER WITH POTATOES AND PEPPERS

SERVES 4

1 POUND RED SNAPPER FILLETS

¼ CUP PLUS 2 TABLESPOONS FRESH LIME JUICE

1 POUND SMALL UNPEELED RED POTATOES, HALVED

1 LARGE RED BELL PEPPER, CUT INTO THIN SLIVERS

2 GARLIC CLOVES, MINCED

2 QUARTER-SIZE SLICES FRESH GINGER, MINCED

2 TABLESPOONS CHOPPED CILANTRO

2 TABLESPOONS VEGETABLE OIL

1 TABLESPOON PLUS 1 TEASPOON GRATED LIME ZEST

½ TEASPOON SALT

¼ TEASPOON BLACK PEPPER

1. Place the fish fillets in one layer in a shallow dish and pour the lime juice on top. Set aside to marinate at room temperature while you prepare the vegetables.

2. In a vegetable steamer, steam the potatoes until they are just tender, about 15 minutes. About 2 minutes before they are done, add the bell pepper and cook until the potatoes are done and the pepper is softened.

3. Preheat the broiler. Line a broiler pan with foil; lightly oil it.

4. In a small bowl, combine the garlic, ginger, cilantro, oil, lime zest, salt, black pepper, and red pepper flakes.

5. Reserving the marinade, transfer the fish, skin-side up, to the broiler pan. Add the reserved marinade to the garlic-ginger mixture.

6. Surround the fish with the steamed potatoes and bell pepper. Spoon all of the marinade mixture over the fish and vegetables, and broil 4 inches from the heat for about 8 minutes, or until the fish just flakes when tested with a fork. About halfway through the cooking, baste the fish and vegetables with the pan juices.

BROILED SCROD
WITH RED PEPPER BUTTER

SERVES 4

1½ CUPS DRY WHITE WINE
1 MEDIUM SHALLOT, SLICED
1 LARGE RED BELL PEPPER
1½ POUNDS SCROD, COD, OR
   HADDOCK FILLETS
2 TABLESPOONS OLIVE OIL

½ TEASPOON SALT
1 TABLESPOON WHITE WINE VINEGAR
1 STICK PLUS 2 TABLESPOONS
   UNSALTED BUTTER, CUT INTO PIECES
¼ TEASPOON GROUND WHITE PEPPER

1. In a medium saucepan, combine the wine, shallot, and bell pepper. Boil uncovered over high heat until no more than 2 tablespoons of liquid remain in the pan, about 10 minutes. Remove from the heat and set aside to cool slightly.

2. Meanwhile, cut the fish into 4 equal serving portions. Rub both sides of the fish with the oil and sprinkle with ¼ teaspoon of the salt.

3. Transfer the bell pepper and liquid to a food processor or blender and process until smooth. Return the mixture to the saucepan. Stir in the vinegar and the remaining ¼ teaspoon salt. Add 1 stick of the butter, a piece at a time, whisking constantly over low heat until the butter melts, about 5 minutes.

4. Strain the sauce into a medium bowl, using a spoon to push the pepper purée through the mesh. Wipe the saucepan clean, pour the strained red pepper butter into it, and set aside.

5. Preheat the broiler with the broiler rack set 4 inches from the heat. Place the fish on the hot broiler rack and broil for 5 to 6 minutes, or until the fish is opaque.

6. Just before serving, gently reheat the red pepper butter and whisk in the remaining 2 tablespoons butter a piece at a time. Stir in the white pepper.

7. To serve, spoon about ¼ cup of the red pepper butter onto each dinner plate and top with the fish.

MARINATED RED SNAPPER

SERVES 4

2-INCH PIECE OF FRESH GINGER,
   GRATED

3 TO 4 GARLIC CLOVES, MINCED

¼ CUP CHOPPED CILANTRO

¼ CUP FRESH LIME JUICE, PLUS
   1 LIME, CUT INTO 8 WEDGES

1 TABLESPOON TEQUILA (OPTIONAL)

¼ TEASPOON RED PEPPER FLAKES

3 TABLESPOONS OLIVE OIL

4 RED SNAPPER OR FLOUNDER FILLETS
   (ABOUT 2 POUNDS TOTAL)

¼ TEASPOON BLACK PEPPER

½ TEASPOON CHILI POWDER

6 RADISHES, THINLY SLICED
   (OPTIONAL)

1. In a baking dish large enough to hold all the fish in one layer, combine the ginger, garlic, cilantro, lime juice, tequila (if using), and red pepper flakes. Add the oil and stir to blend. Place the fish in the dish, turning once to coat with the marinade. Cover with plastic wrap and marinate at room temperature for 30 to 40 minutes, turning occasionally.

2. Preheat the broiler. Line a broiler pan with foil.

3. Arrange the fillets in a single layer on the prepared broiler pan and broil 4 inches from the heat for 3 to 6 minutes per side, or until the fish just flakes when tested with a fork. Watch the fish carefully to prevent overcooking, the longer it has marinated, the more rapidly it will cook.

4. Transfer the fish fillets to individual dinner plates and sprinkle with the black pepper and chili powder. Serve with the lime wedges and radish slices, if desired.

COD STEAKS TOPPED WITH TOMATO AND BASIL

SERVES 4

◇ LOW-FAT

2 TEASPOONS OLIVE OIL

1 POUND TOMATOES, COARSELY CHOPPED

¾ CUP (LOOSELY PACKED) BASIL LEAVES, CHOPPED

3 TABLESPOONS MEDIUM-DRY SHERRY

⅛ TEASPOON SALT

¼ TEASPOON BLACK PEPPER

4 COD STEAKS, CENTRAL BONES REMOVED (ABOUT 1¼ POUNDS TOTAL)

1. Preheat the grill. Cut out four 12 x 16-inch pieces of heavy-duty foil. Brush the olive oil over the foil.

2. In a bowl, combine the tomatoes with the basil and sherry, and season the mixture with the salt and pepper.

3. Lay a cod steak in the center of each piece of foil and top it with one-fourth of the tomato mixture. Bring the two short sides of the foil together and fold over as you would to wrap a sandwich. Fold in the ends to seal the packets.

4. Place the packets on the grill and cook for 3 to 5 minutes. Carefully turn and cook for 5 minutes on the second side.

5. Unwrap the packets with the tomato-side up and slide the contents of each one onto an individual plate. Remove and discard the thin strips of cod skin and serve the steaks at once.

GRILLED SALMON STEAKS WITH FRESH DILL AND THYME

SERVES 4

4 SALMON STEAKS (ABOUT 2 POUNDS
  TOTAL)
3 TABLESPOONS CHOPPED FRESH DILL,
  OR 1 TABLESPOON DRIED
3 TABLESPOONS CHOPPED FRESH
  THYME, OR 1 TABLESPOON DRIED

1 TABLESPOON GRATED LEMON ZEST,
  PLUS 1 LEMON, CUT INTO WEDGES
4 TABLESPOONS UNSALTED BUTTER
¼ TEASPOON SALT
¼ TEASPOON BLACK PEPPER

1. Sprinkle both sides of the salmon steaks with the dill, thyme, and lemon zest.

2. Prepare the grill. Cut out four 12-inch squares of heavy-duty foil

3. Place 1 salmon steak on each piece of foil and top with 1 tablespoon butter. Bring the edges of the foil together and crimp well to keep the juices in the packets.

4. Place the packets on the grill and cook for 5 minutes. Carefully turn and cook for 5 minutes on the second side.

5. Open the packets, season with the salt and pepper, and serve with the lemon wedges.

KITCHEN NOTE: *When it's not grilling season, you can bake the packets of herbed fish in a 425° oven. Place the packets on a baking sheet or jelly-roll pan, and bake them without turning.*

BROILED SALMON WITH GREEN SAUCE

SERVES 4

¼ CUP FRESH LEMON JUICE, PLUS
    1 LEMON, CUT INTO WEDGES
3 TABLESPOONS OLIVE OIL
2 TABLESPOONS UNSALTED BUTTER
2 ANCHOVY FILLETS
6 PARSLEY SPRIGS
1 GARLIC CLOVE, LIGHTLY CRUSHED
    AND PEELED

1 TABLESPOON PLUS 1 TEASPOON
    CAPERS, RINSED AND DRAINED
1 TEASPOON FRESH OR DRIED
    ROSEMARY
¼ TEASPOON BLACK PEPPER
⅛ TEASPOON SALT
4 SALMON STEAKS (½ INCH THICK,
    ABOUT 2 POUNDS TOTAL)

1. Preheat the broiler.

2. In a food processor or blender, combine the lemon juice, 2 tablespoons of the oil, the butter, anchovies, parsley, garlic, capers, rosemary, pepper, and salt, and process until smooth and well blended.

3. Coat the salmon steaks on both sides with the remaining 1 tablespoon oil. Place the steaks on a broiler pan and broil 4 inches

from the heat for 3 to 4 minutes. Turn and broil for 4 minutes, or until the salmon is slightly golden and just flakes when tested with a fork.

4. Divide the salmon steaks among 4 dinner plates and top with a generous tablespoonful of green sauce. Serve with the lemon wedges.

KITCHEN NOTE: *The green sauce for this broiled salmon is a Mediterranean-style sauce made with anchovies, capers, lemon, garlic, parsley, and rosemary. Its pungent flavors are a wonderful counterpoint to the delicate flavors of fish and shellfish. Make a double or triple batch of the sauce and keep it on hand for impromptu grilling. Keep it well covered and refrigerated.*

LEMON-MARINATED SWORDFISH KEBABS

SERVES 4

¼ CUP FRESH LEMON JUICE, PLUS 2
  LEMONS, CUT INTO 6 WEDGES EACH
1 TABLESPOON GRATED LEMON ZEST
3 TABLESPOONS EXTRA-VIRGIN OLIVE
  OIL

15 LARGE BAY LEAVES
¼ TEASPOON BLACK PEPPER
4 SWORDFISH STEAKS (1¼ INCHES
  THICK, ABOUT 1½ POUNDS TOTAL),
  CUT INTO 16 CUBES

1. In a dish large enough to hold the sword-fish steaks in one layer, combine the lemon juice, lemon zest, oil, 3 of the bay leaves, and the pepper.

2. Add the swordfish to the marinade and toss to coat well. Cover the dish with plastic wrap and refrigerate for at least 30 minutes.

3. Preheat the broiler. Thread the swordfish cubes alternately with lemon wedges and the remaining 12 bay leaves on four 15-inch skewers. Balance the skewers lengthwise on a 13 x 9 x 2-inch flameproof baking pan. Drizzle the kebabs with the marinade and broil 4 inches from the heat for 5 minutes. Turn the skewers over and broil for 5 minutes, or until the fish just flakes when tested with a fork.

4. Divide the kebabs among 4 dinner plates and serve.

97

Swordfish with Spicy Tomato-Orange Sauce

SERVES 4

½ CUP OLIVE OIL

1 SMALL RED ONION, FINELY CHOPPED

3 GARLIC CLOVES, MINCED

1 TABLESPOON MINCED FRESH BASIL, OR 1 TEASPOON DRIED

2 TEASPOONS RED PEPPER FLAKES

½ CUP DRY WHITE WINE OR DRY VERMOUTH

½ CUP ORANGE JUICE, PLUS 1 ORANGE, PEELED AND CUT INTO SECTIONS

3 TABLESPOONS FRESH LEMON JUICE

3 MEDIUM TOMATOES, COARSELY CHOPPED

2 TABLESPOONS CHOPPED PARSLEY

½ TEASPOON SALT

¼ TEASPOON BLACK PEPPER

4 SWORDFISH STEAKS (½ TO ¾ INCH THICK)

3 SCALLIONS, CHOPPED

1. Preheat the broiler.

2. In a large skillet, warm ¼ cup of the oil over medium heat. Add the onion, garlic, basil, and red pepper flakes, and cook, stirring, until the onion is softened but not browned, about 5 minutes.

3. Add the wine, orange juice, and lemon juice; increase the heat to high and boil until reduced to a syrup, 4 to 6 minutes.

4. Add the tomatoes and cook just until heated through, about 1 minute. Stir in the parsley, salt, and pepper; cover and remove from the heat.

5. Arrange the swordfish on a broiler pan and brush each with 1 tablespoon of the oil.

6. Broil the swordfish 2 to 3 inches from the heat for about 5 minutes per side (depending on the thickness), until almost opaque.

7. Spoon some sauce onto a broilerproof serving platter and arrange the fish on top. Spoon more sauce over the fish and top with the orange sections and scallions. Set the platter under the broiler to heat the oranges and allow the fish to finish cooking, about 2 minutes. Serve hot.

BROILED TUNA WITH ORANGE-CUMIN SAUCE

SERVES 4

¼ CUP CUMIN SEEDS

1 CUP ORANGE JUICE, PLUS 1 ORANGE, THINLY SLICED

1 TABLESPOON DARK BROWN SUGAR

4 TUNA FILLETS (¾ INCH THICK)

¼ CUP OLIVE OIL

1. In a small skillet, toast the cumin seeds over medium heat until fragrant, about 2 minutes. Shake the skillet from time to time to keep the seeds from scorching. Grind the seeds with a mortar and pestle or place between 2 sheets of wax paper and crush with a rolling pin.

2. In a small saucepan, combine the orange juice, cumin, and sugar, and bring to a boil over high heat. Cook until reduced to ½ cup, about 5 minutes.

3. Meanwhile, preheat the broiler.

4. Place the fish on a broiler pan and brush on both sides with the oil. Broil 4 to 5 inches from the heat for 3 to 4 minutes per side.

5. Transfer the fillets to a platter and top with the sauce. Garnish with the orange slices.

KITCHEN NOTE: *Pan-toasting spices brings their flavor to its peak in the same way that roasting enhances nuts or coffee. Be careful not to scorch the cumin, though: As soon as the spice is fragrant, tip the seeds out of the hot pan so they do not continue to cook. If you do not have cumin seeds on hand, you can substitute ground cumin; and it, too, will benefit from a light toasting.*

SCALLOP AND VEGETABLE SKEWERS WITH GARLIC BUTTER

SERVES 4

3 TABLESPOONS UNSALTED BUTTER
3 GARLIC CLOVES, MINCED
1 TEASPOON FRESH LEMON JUICE
¼ TEASPOON RED PEPPER FLAKES
3 TABLESPOONS CHOPPED PARSLEY
2 TEASPOONS GRATED LEMON ZEST
1 POUND SEA SCALLOPS, HALVED IF
    LARGE

1 LARGE YELLOW SQUASH, HALVED
    LENGTHWISE AND CUT CROSSWISE
    INTO ½-INCH-THICK HALF-ROUNDS
1 LARGE GREEN BELL PEPPER, CUT INTO
    1-INCH SQUARES
16 CHERRY TOMATOES

1. Preheat the broiler or prepare the grill. If broiling, line a broiler pan with foil.

2. In a small skillet or saucepan, warm the butter over medium heat until it is melted. Add the garlic and cook until fragrant, about 3 minutes. Remove from the heat and stir in the lemon juice, red pepper flakes, parsley, and lemon zest.

3. Alternating ingredients, thread the scallops, squash, bell pepper, and tomatoes on skewers. (If broiling, place the skewers on the broiler pan.) Brush the skewers with half the garlic butter, and grill or broil 4 inches from the heat for about 4 minutes.

4. Turn the skewers over, brush with the remaining garlic butter, and grill or broil until the scallops are cooked through and the vegetables are tender, about 4 minutes.

GRILLED SHRIMP WITH TOMATO-GINGER SAUCE

SERVES 4

1 ONION, CHOPPED

½ CUP DRY WHITE WINE

2 TABLESPOONS FRESH LEMON JUICE

2 TABLESPOONS OLIVE OIL

24 MEDIUM SHRIMP, SHELLED AND DEVEINED

3 SCALLIONS, CHOPPED

6 GARLIC CLOVES, MINCED

1 TABLESPOON MINCED FRESH GINGER

2 JALAPEÑO PEPPERS, SEEDED AND CHOPPED

¼ TEASPOON GROUND CORIANDER

¼ TEASPOON CUMIN

¼ TEASPOON DRY MUSTARD

3 TOMATOES, COARSELY CHOPPED

1 TABLESPOON RED WINE VINEGAR

1 TEASPOON BROWN SUGAR

1. In a bowl, combine the onion, wine, lemon juice, and 1 tablespoon of the oil. Add the shrimp and let them marinate in the refrigerator for 30 minutes to 1 hour.

2. Meanwhile, in a large skillet, warm the remaining 1 tablespoon oil over medium-high heat. Add the scallions, garlic, ginger, and jalapeños, and cook for 2 minutes, stirring constantly. Stir in the coriander, cumin, and mustard, and cook the mixture for 1 minute.

3. Add the tomatoes and cook, stirring constantly, for 1 minute. Remove the skillet from

the heat and stir in the vinegar and brown sugar. Transfer the sauce to a serving bowl and let it cool.

4. Preheat the broiler. Thread the shrimp in interlocking pairs onto 4 skewers. Brush the shrimp with any remaining marinade and broil them about 2 inches from the heat until they are opaque, about 3 minutes.

5. Serve the shrimp on their skewers with the sauce presented alongside.

Broiled Shrimp with Cilantro-Citrus Butter

SERVES 4

½ TEASPOON CURRY POWDER

1½ TEASPOONS HOT PEPPER SAUCE

1 EGG

1 CUP FINE UNSEASONED DRY BREAD
CRUMBS

1½ POUNDS MEDIUM SHRIMP, SHELLED
AND DEVEINED

2 TABLESPOONS OLIVE OIL

1 STICK PLUS 2 TABLESPOONS
UNSALTED BUTTER, CUT INTO SMALL
PIECES

¾ CUP ORANGE JUICE

3 TABLESPOONS FRESH LIME JUICE

3 TABLESPOONS GRATED ORANGE ZEST

3 TABLESPOONS CHOPPED CILANTRO

1 TABLESPOON HONEY

½ TEASPOON SALT

3 CUPS COARSELY SHREDDED ROMAINE
LETTUCE

1. Preheat the broiler. Lightly oil a medium roasting pan.

2. In a small bowl, blend the curry powder and 1 teaspoon of the hot pepper sauce. Add the egg and beat thoroughly. Place the bread crumbs in a separate small bowl.

3. Dip the shrimp first in the egg mixture, then in the bread crumbs, coating them evenly. Arrange them in a single layer in the prepared roasting pan, leaving space between them. Drizzle the breaded shrimp with the oil and dot with 4 tablespoons of the butter.

4. Broil the shrimp, turning once, for 7 minutes, or until cooked through and golden. Transfer the shrimp to a platter and cover loosely with foil to keep warm.

5. Place the roasting pan on top of the stove over low heat. Add the orange and lime juices, orange zest, cilantro, honey, salt, and remaining ½ teaspoon hot pepper sauce. Add the remaining 6 tablespoons butter a piece at a time, stirring well to incorporate each piece.

6. Surround the shrimp with the shredded lettuce and serve the sauce on the side.

BROILED CRAB-POTATO PATTIES

SERVES 4

1 POUND ALL-PURPOSE POTATOES

1 POUND LUMP CRABMEAT, PICKED
OVER

¾ CUP FINELY CHOPPED ONION

½ CUP FINELY CHOPPED PARSLEY

3 TABLESPOONS MINCED DILL

1 TABLESPOON DRY SHERRY

2 TABLESPOONS PLAIN LOW-FAT
YOGURT

2 EGG WHITES, BEATEN

¼ TEASPOON SALT

¼ TEASPOON BLACK PEPPER

¼ TEASPOON GROUND MACE OR
NUTMEG

⅛ TEASPOON CAYENNE PEPPER

¾ CUP FINE UNSEASONED DRY BREAD
CRUMBS

2 TABLESPOONS OLIVE OIL

1 TABLESPOON UNSALTED BUTTER

2 LEMONS, CUT INTO WEDGES

1. In a large pot of boiling water, cook the potatoes until tender. When cool enough to handle, peel them and grate them through the large holes of a hand-held grater.

2. Preheat the broiler. Lightly oil a broiler rack.

3. In a large mixing bowl, combine the potatoes, crabmeat, onion, parsley, dill, sherry, yogurt, egg whites, salt, pepper, mace, and cayenne, and mix gently to combine.

4. Form the mixture into 12 patties about ½ inch thick. Dredge each patty in the bread crumbs to coat it completely and place on the prepared broiler rack.

5. In a small saucepan, warm the oil with the butter over low heat until the butter is melted. Drizzle half of this mixture over the tops of the patties and broil until they turn a crusty golden brown, 3 to 5 minutes. Turn the patties over, drizzle the remaining butter mixture over them, and broil for 3 to 5 minutes. Serve hot with the lemon wedges.

GRILLED FISH SALAD

SERVES 4

◆ EXTRA-QUICK

4 QUARTER-SIZE SLICES FRESH GINGER, FINELY CHOPPED

2 GARLIC CLOVES, FINELY CHOPPED

¼ CUP REDUCED-SODIUM SOY SAUCE

3 TABLESPOONS FRESH LIME JUICE

2 TABLESPOONS VEGETABLE OIL

1 TABLESPOON HONEY

1 TEASPOON GRATED LIME ZEST

¼ TEASPOON BLACK PEPPER

¼ TEASPOON RED PEPPER FLAKES

1¼ POUNDS COD OR HALIBUT STEAKS

4 CUPS SHREDDED NAPA CABBAGE

4 CUPS SHREDDED RED LEAF LETTUCE

2 LARGE CARROTS, CUT INTO THIN MATCHSTICKS

2 CUPS BEAN SPROUTS

2 TABLESPOONS SESAME SEEDS, TOASTED IF DESIRED

1. Preheat the broiler or prepare the grill. If broiling, line a broiler pan with foil and lightly oil the foil.

2. In a medium bowl, combine the ginger, garlic, soy sauce, lime juice, oil, honey, lime zest, black pepper, and red pepper flakes, and whisk to blend. Set aside half of the mixture to use as a salad dressing.

3. Place the fish on the grill or broiler pan and baste with half of the marinade. Grill or broil 4 inches from the heat for 5 minutes.

Turn the fish over and brush with the remaining marinade. Cook until the fish just flakes when tested with a fork, about 5 minutes.

4. Meanwhile, divide the cabbage, lettuce, carrots, and bean sprouts evenly among 4 dinner plates.

5. Cut the hot fish into ¾-inch chunks and place them on top of the greens. Pour the dressing over all. Sprinkle with the sesame seeds.

SALMON-RICE SALAD
WITH LEMON-PEPPER DRESSING

SERVES 4

1 CUP CHICKEN BROTH, PREFERABLY
   REDUCED-SODIUM

1 CUP RICE

2 GARLIC CLOVES, MINCED

⅓ CUP FRESH LEMON JUICE

¼ CUP OLIVE OIL

1 TABLESPOON DIJON MUSTARD

½ TEASPOON BLACK PEPPER

¼ TEASPOON SALT

1 LARGE YELLOW OR GREEN BELL
   PEPPER, CUT INTO BITE-SIZE PIECES

1 PINT CHERRY TOMATOES, HALVED

4 SCALLIONS, COARSELY CHOPPED

¼ CUP CHOPPED FRESH DILL, OR
   2 TEASPOONS DRIED

ONE 6½-OUNCE CAN SALMON,
   DRAINED

1 SMALL HEAD OF BOSTON OR ICEBERG
   LETTUCE, SEPARATED INTO LEAVES

1. In a medium saucepan, bring the chicken broth and 1 cup of water to a boil. Add the rice and garlic, reduce the heat to low, cover, and simmer until the rice is tender and all the liquid is absorbed, about 20 minutes. When the rice is done, remove it from the heat and turn it into a large bowl to cool slightly; fluff the rice with a fork or spoon to separate the grains and speed the cooling.

2. Meanwhile, in a small bowl, combine the lemon juice, olive oil, mustard, black pepper, and salt.

3. When the rice has cooled slightly, add the lemon-pepper dressing, the bell pepper, tomatoes, scallions, and dill. Flake the salmon into the bowl and toss lightly to combine.

4. Serve the salad mounded in lettuce leaves.

Zesty Tuna
with Mexican Seasonings

SERVES 4

◆ EXTRA-QUICK ◇ LOW-FAT

4 CORN TORTILLAS, CUT INTO ¼-INCH-
WIDE STRIPS

ONE 6½-OUNCE CAN WATER-PACKED
TUNA, DRAINED

3 MEDIUM PLUM TOMATOES, COARSELY
CHOPPED

2 MEDIUM CARROTS, COARSELY
CHOPPED

4 SCALLIONS, COARSELY CHOPPED

¼ CUP CHOPPED CILANTRO

3½ TABLESPOONS FRESH LIME JUICE

1 TABLESPOON OLIVE OIL

3 DROPS OF HOT PEPPER SAUCE

1 GARLIC CLOVE, MINCED

1½ TEASPOONS GRATED LIME ZEST

¾ TEASPOON OREGANO

½ TEASPOON CUMIN

½ TEASPOON SALT

¼ TEASPOON BLACK PEPPER

8 BOSTON, BIBB, OR BUTTERCRUNCH
LETTUCE LEAVES

½ CUP PLAIN LOW-FAT YOGURT

1. Preheat the oven to 375°. Place the tortilla strips on a baking sheet and bake for 10 minutes, or until crisp.

2. Meanwhile, flake the tuna into a large bowl. Add the tomatoes, carrots, scallions, and cilantro, and toss together.

3. In a small bowl, combine the lime juice, oil, hot pepper sauce, garlic, lime zest, oreg-

ano, cumin, salt, and pepper. Pour the dressing over the tuna and vegetables, and toss to distribute the dressing.

4. Place the lettuce leaves on a platter. Divide the tuna mixture among the lettuce leaves. Serve 2 lettuce cups per person and top each with tortilla strips and 1 tablespoon of yogurt.

Tuna-Spinach Salad with Peanut Dressing

SERVES 6

◆ EXTRA-QUICK

2 TABLESPOONS CREAMY PEANUT BUTTER

2 TABLESPOONS REDUCED-SODIUM SOY SAUCE

2 TEASPOONS GROUND GINGER

⅔ CUP ORANGE JUICE

3 TABLESPOONS GRATED ORANGE ZEST

2 TABLESPOONS CIDER VINEGAR

1 TABLESPOON ORIENTAL (DARK) SESAME OIL

¼ TEASPOON BLACK PEPPER

8 CUPS (PACKED) FRESH SPINACH LEAVES, TORN INTO BITE-SIZE PIECES

¼ POUND MUSHROOMS, SLICED

2 MEDIUM CARROTS, CUT INTO THIN MATCHSTICKS

1 SMALL RED ONION, THINLY SLICED

1½ CUPS BEAN SPROUTS

ONE 12-OUNCE CAN WATER-PACKED TUNA, DRAINED

¼ CUP CHOPPED CILANTRO

1. In a small bowl, blend the peanut butter, soy sauce, and ground ginger. Stir in the orange juice and zest, the vinegar, sesame oil, and pepper.

2. Mound the spinach, mushrooms, carrots, onion, and bean sprouts on 4 individual salad plates or a single serving platter. Flake the tuna on top.

3. Stir the cilantro into the dressing. Spoon the dressing over the salad.

Tuna Salad Niçoise

SERVES 6

1 POUND SMALL UNPEELED RED
  POTATOES, QUARTERED

2 EGGS

¾ POUND FRESH GREEN BEANS, OR ONE
  10-OUNCE PACKAGE FROZEN CUT
  GREEN BEANS, THAWED

¼ CUP WHITE WINE VINEGAR OR CIDER
  VINEGAR

⅓ CUP OLIVE OIL

1 TABLESPOON DIJON MUSTARD

1 GARLIC CLOVE, MINCED

1 TEASPOON BASIL

½ TEASPOON SALT

¼ TEASPOON BLACK PEPPER

1 PINT CHERRY TOMATOES, HALVED

ONE 6-OUNCE CAN PITTED BLACK
  OLIVES, DRAINED

ONE 6½-OUNCE CAN WATER-PACKED
  TUNA, DRAINED

1. Place the potatoes and eggs in a large saucepan and cover with cold water. Bring to a boil over medium-high heat. Reduce the heat to medium and simmer, uncovered, until the potatoes just test tender, about 20 minutes. Remove the eggs after 15 minutes of cooking, cool them under cold running water, then peel them and finely chop.

2. Meanwhile, cut the fresh beans into 2-inch lengths.

3. When the potatoes are just tender, add the beans (fresh or thawed frozen) to the saucepan and continue cooking the potatoes and

beans for about 2 minutes, or until the beans are just crisp-tender. Drain the potatoes and beans.

4. In a small bowl, whisk together the vinegar, oil, mustard, garlic, basil, salt, and pepper. Place the still-warm potatoes and beans in a serving bowl and pour the dressing over them. Toss to coat well.

5. Add the cherry tomatoes and olives to the bowl. Flake the tuna into the bowl with a fork. Toss gently to combine all the ingredients. Sprinkle the chopped egg on top.

SHRIMP AND GREEN BEAN SALAD

SERVES 4

TWO 10-OUNCE PACKAGES FROZEN
CUT GREEN BEANS

1 POUND MEDIUM SHRIMP, IN THE
SHELL

1½ TABLESPOONS VINEGAR,
PREFERABLY TARRAGON

1 TABLESPOON OLIVE OIL

2 TABLESPOONS CHOPPED FRESH
TARRAGON, OR 2 TEASPOONS DRIED

2 TABLESPOONS MINCED CHIVES OR
SCALLION GREENS

¼ TEASPOON SALT

¼ TEASPOON BLACK PEPPER

½ CUP PLAIN LOW-FAT YOGURT

1 TABLESPOON SOUR CREAM

1½ TEASPOONS DIJON MUSTARD

1 TEASPOON TOMATO PASTE

1 TABLESPOON CHOPPED PARSLEY

1. In a large saucepan of boiling water, cook the beans just until heated through, about 2 minutes. Keeping the water in the saucepan at a simmer for cooking the shrimp, use a slotted spoon to transfer the beans to a strainer; refresh them under cold running water, pat dry, and transfer to a bowl. Set aside.

2. Add the shrimp to the saucepan. Cover the pan and simmer the shrimp until they are opaque, 2 to 3 minutes. Drain the shrimp; when they are cool enough to handle, shell and devein them. Add the shrimp to the beans.

3. In a small bowl, whisk together the vinegar, oil, half of the tarragon, 1 tablespoon of the chives, and ⅛ teaspoon each of the salt and pepper.

4. Arrange the shrimp and beans on a serving platter and spoon the vinegar-and-oil marinade over it. Let the dish marinate at room temperature for 30 minutes.

5. Shortly before serving, combine the yogurt, sour cream, mustard, tomato paste, parsley, and the remaining tarragon, 1 tablespoon chives, and ⅛ teaspoon each salt and pepper. Pour the dressing into a small serving bowl and serve it alongside the salad.

Asian Crab-and-Vegetable Salad

SERVES 4

1 POUND LUMP CRABMEAT, PICKED OVER

¼ CUP FRESH LEMON JUICE

¼ TEASPOON SALT

¼ TEASPOON BLACK PEPPER

1 TEASPOON DRY MUSTARD

2 TABLESPOONS GRATED FRESH GINGER

2 TEASPOONS RICE WINE VINEGAR

1 GARLIC CLOVE, MINCED

2 TABLESPOONS DRY WHITE WINE

2 TABLESPOONS VEGETABLE OIL, PREFERABLY PEANUT

¼ TEASPOON ORIENTAL (DARK) SESAME OIL

1 SMALL CUCUMBER—PEELED, HALVED LENGTHWISE, SEEDED, AND SLICED

1 CUP CANNED SLICED BAMBOO SHOOTS, RINSED AND DRAINED

1 CUP CANNED SLICED WATER CHESTNUTS, DRAINED

¼ POUND SNOW PEAS, CUT INTO THIN SLIVERS

2 TABLESPOONS CHOPPED PIMIENTO (OPTIONAL)

2 HEADS OF BOSTON LETTUCE, SEPARATED INTO LEAVES

1. In a large bowl, combine the crabmeat with the lemon juice and ⅛ teaspoon each of the salt and pepper. Refrigerate the mixture while you assemble the remaining ingredients for the salad.

2. Place the mustard in a bowl. Place the ginger in a piece of cheesecloth and squeeze it over the bowl to extract the juice; discard the ginger. Pour in the rice wine vinegar and whisk well, then add the garlic and wine, and whisk again. Let the mixture stand for 5 minutes before whisking in the vegetable oil and

sesame oil. Add the remaining ⅛ teaspoon each salt and pepper. Set the dressing aside.

3. Add the cucumber, bamboo shoots, water chestnuts, snow peas, and pimiento (if using) to the crabmeat, and mix well. Pour the dressing over the salad and toss gently. Chill the salad for 30 minutes.

4. To serve, arrange the lettuce leaves on individual plates. Spoon the salad into the leaves and serve immediately.

Mixed Seafood Chowder

SERVES 4

¾ POUND FLOUNDER FILLET, CUT INTO
¾-INCH PIECES

½ POUND HALIBUT, GROUPER, OR COD
FILLETS, CUT INTO ½-INCH PIECES

½ POUND MEDIUM SHRIMP—SHELLED,
DEVEINED, AND HALVED
LENGTHWISE

2 TABLESPOONS FRESH LEMON JUICE

4 TABLESPOONS UNSALTED BUTTER

¼ CUP FLOUR

1 TEASPOON CURRY POWDER

2 CUPS FISH BROTH, BOTTLED CLAM
JUICE, OR REDUCED-SODIUM
CHICKEN BROTH

2 CUPS REDUCED-SODIUM CHICKEN
BROTH

½ TEASPOON SALT

¾ TEASPOON BLACK PEPPER

½ CUP FROZEN TINY PEAS, THAWED

½ CUP HALF-AND-HALF

2 TABLESPOONS MINCED FRESH DILL,
OR 1 TEASPOON DRIED

1. In a medium bowl, combine the fish and shrimp, sprinkle with the lemon juice, and toss gently. Set aside.

2. In a large saucepan, warm the butter over medium-low heat until melted. Add the flour and curry powder, and cook, whisking constantly, until the flour is completely blended, about 3 minutes.

3. Whisking constantly, gradually add the fish broth and chicken broth. Add the salt and pepper, increase the heat to medium-high, and bring the mixture to a boil, whisk-

ing occasionally. Reduce the heat to low, cover, and simmer for 10 minutes.

4. Add the fish and shrimp mixture, the peas, and cream, stir to combine, and simmer until the fish and shrimp are opaque, about 3 minutes. Remove the pan from the heat and stir in the dill.

5. Ladle the chowder into 4 soup bowls and serve hot.

LIGHT SEAFOOD NEWBURG

SERVES 4

1 CUP CHICKEN BROTH, PREFERABLY
REDUCED-SODIUM

3 TABLESPOONS SHERRY, DRY WHITE
WINE, OR CHICKEN BROTH

PINCH OF CAYENNE PEPPER

2 GARLIC CLOVES, MINCED

4 SCALLIONS, COARSELY CHOPPED,
GREEN AND WHITE PARTS KEPT
SEPARATE

½ POUND MEDIUM SHRIMP, SHELLED
AND DEVEINED

½ POUND SEA SCALLOPS, HALVED IF
LARGE

3 TABLESPOONS UNSALTED BUTTER

¼ CUP FLOUR

½ CUP LOW-FAT MILK

ONE 6-OUNCE CAN CRABMEAT,
DRAINED

1. In a medium saucepan, combine the broth, sherry, cayenne, garlic, and scallion whites. Cover and bring to a boil over medium-high heat.

2. Add the shrimp and scallops, and cook just until the liquid returns to a boil, then remove from the heat. Reserving the broth, use a slotted spoon to transfer the shrimp, scallops, and scallion whites to a plate. Cover the seafood mixture loosely with foil and set aside.

3. In another medium saucepan, warm the butter over medium heat until melted. Stir in the flour and cook, stirring, until the flour is no longer visible, about 1 minute. Gradually whisk in the reserved broth until smooth. Whisk in the milk until well combined.

4. Return the shrimp, scallops, and scallion whites to the sauce. Gently stir in the crabmeat and scallion greens. Cook, stirring gently, until the seafood is just cooked through, about 3 minutes.

Mussels Marinière

SERVES 4

3 TABLESPOONS UNSALTED BUTTER

1 MEDIUM ONION, COARSELY CHOPPED

3 GARLIC CLOVES, MINCED

1 CUP DRY WHITE WINE

½ TEASPOON BLACK PEPPER

4 POUNDS MUSSELS, SCRUBBED AND
DEBEARDED

3 TABLESPOONS CHOPPED PARSLEY
(OPTIONAL)

1. In a large saucepan, warm the butter over medium-high heat until it is melted. Add the onion and garlic, and cook until the onion is translucent, about 5 minutes.

2. Add the wine and pepper, and bring to a boil over high heat. Add the mussels, return to a boil, cover, and cook over high heat, shaking the pan occasionally, until all of the mussels have opened, about 8 minutes. Discard any mussels that fail to open.

3. Dividing evenly, transfer the mussels to individual serving bowls. Stir the parsley (if using) into the broth in the saucepan and pour the broth over the mussels.

KITCHEN NOTE: *You'll need to clean the mussels before steaming them, and this should be done as close to cooking time as possible. Scrub the shells with a stiff brush under cold running water, then pull off the "beards"—the dark fibers that protrude from the shells.*

STEAMED SPICED CRABS

SERVES 4

◇ LOW-FAT

¼ CUP MINCED FRESH GINGER

1 WHOLE GARLIC BULB, THE CLOVES
PEELED AND CHOPPED

1 TABLESPOON MUSTARD SEEDS

½ TEASPOON ALLSPICE

2 TEASPOONS RED PEPPER FLAKES

6 BAY LEAVES, CRUMBLED

1 TABLESPOON FENNEL SEEDS

2 ONIONS, FINELY CHOPPED

1 CUP CIDER VINEGAR

1 CUP DRY WHITE WINE

12 LIVE BLUE CRABS

1. In a medium bowl, combine the ginger, garlic, mustard seeds, allspice, red pepper flakes, bay leaves, fennel seeds, and onions.

2. Set a steamer insert in a tall stockpot and pour in the vinegar, wine, and 2 cups of water. Bring the liquid to a boil, then remove the pot from the heat.

3. Put three crabs in the steamer and scatter one-fourth of the spice-and-onion mixture over them. Continue the layering, with three crabs and one-fourth of the spice mixture in each layer. Cover the pot tightly and set it over high heat.

4. Steam the crabs for 20 minutes, timing from the moment when the steam first escapes from the pot. At the end of the steaming period, turn off the heat, and let the pot stand, still covered, while the steam subsides, about 3 minutes.

5. Serve the crabs hot, providing a mallet for cracking the claws, nutpicks for extracting the meat, and plenty of napkins.

KITCHEN NOTE: *If you happen to have whole allspice berries, use them in place of the ground allspice. Use a full teaspoon of them and lightly crack them under the broad side of a knife first.*

Pan-Blackened Red Snapper

SERVES 4

2 CUPS COARSELY CHOPPED TOMATOES

½ CUP DRY WHITE WINE

¼ CUP FRESH LIME JUICE

4 RED SNAPPER FILLETS (½ INCH
   THICK), WITH SKIN

¼ TEASPOON SALT

½ TEASPOON BLACK PEPPER

¾ CUP BEEF BROTH

3 TABLESPOONS MINCED CHIVES OR
   SCALLION GREENS

1 STICK UNSALTED BUTTER—
   4 TABLESPOONS MELTED AND 4
   TABLESPOONS CHILLED

1. In a medium bowl, combine the tomatoes, wine, and lime juice. Place the fillets, flesh-side down, in the marinade. Let marinate at room temperature for 20 to 30 minutes.

2. Reserving the marinade, remove the fish and pat dry with paper towels. Sprinkle the fillets with the salt and pepper.

3. Transfer the marinade to a medium saucepan and bring to a boil over medium-high heat. Boil until reduced by half, about 10 minutes.

4. Stir in the broth and 2 tablespoons of the chives, and boil until syrupy and reduced to 1 cup, about 15 minutes.

5. Reduce the heat to low. Stir in the 4 tablespoons chilled butter, 1 tablespoon at a time (the sauce will thicken as the butter melts). Keep warm over very low heat.

6. Preheat a large cast-iron skillet or 2 medium skillets over high heat. Pour in the 4 tablespoons melted butter. Carefully place the fillets, flesh-side down, in the skillet and cook over high heat for 1 to 2 minutes. Check the edges of the fillets for color; when the fish is very brown, almost black, turn and cook the other side until well browned. Total cooking time will be 6 to 8 minutes, depending on the thickness of the fillets.

7. Divide the fillets among individual plates, top with sauce, and sprinkle with the remaining 1 tablespoon chives.

Beer Batter Fillets with Red Pepper Slaw

SERVES 4

◆ EXTRA-QUICK

3 TABLESPOONS SOUR CREAM

2 TABLESPOONS FRESH LEMON JUICE

2 TEASPOONS GRATED LEMON ZEST
   (OPTIONAL)

½ TEASPOON SALT

¼ TEASPOON BLACK PEPPER

PINCH OF SUGAR

2 LARGE RED BELL PEPPERS, THINLY
   SLICED

1 SMALL RED ONION, THINLY SLICED

¼ CUP CHOPPED PARSLEY (OPTIONAL)

⅔ CUP FLOUR

2 TABLESPOONS CORNMEAL

¾ TEASPOON SALT

¼ TEASPOON CAYENNE PEPPER

1 EGG

⅔ CUP BEER, PREFERABLY DARK

1½ CUPS VEGETABLE OIL

4 SMALL FLOUNDER OR SOLE FILLETS
   (ABOUT 1½ POUNDS TOTAL)

1. In a medium bowl, combine the sour cream, lemon juice, lemon zest (if using), salt, black pepper, and sugar. Add the bell peppers, onion, and parsley (if using). Toss to coat the ingredients well with the dressing.

2. In a shallow bowl, combine the flour, cornmeal, salt, and cayenne. In a small bowl, lightly beat the egg. Stir the beer and beaten egg into the dry ingredients.

3. In a 10-inch skillet, warm the oil over medium heat until very hot but not smoking (about 375° on a deep-fat thermometer).

4. Dip the fish into the batter and add it to the hot oil. Fry until golden brown, about 4 minutes; carefully turn the fish over halfway through. Drain the fish on paper towels.

5. Serve the fish with the red pepper slaw on the side.

CHILI SHRIMP

SERVES 4

2 TABLESPOONS DRY SHERRY

1 TABLESPOON SUGAR

1 TEASPOON RED WINE VINEGAR

1½ TABLESPOONS REDUCED-SODIUM
SOY SAUCE

2 TABLESPOONS CHICKEN BROTH

½ TEASPOON RED PEPPER FLAKES

1 TEASPOON CORNSTARCH

1 POUND LARGE SHRIMP

2½ TABLESPOONS PLUS 2 TEASPOONS
VEGETABLE OIL

2 WHOLE SCALLIONS, CHOPPED

2 TEASPOONS MINCED FRESH GINGER

1 GARLIC CLOVE, MINCED

1 TEASPOON ORIENTAL (DARK) SESAME
OIL

1. In a small bowl, combine the sherry, sugar, vinegar, soy sauce, chicken broth, red pepper flakes, and cornstarch; stir to blend in the cornstarch. Set the seasoning sauce aside.

2. Using a small pair of scissors, cut the shell along the back of shrimp, cutting into the shrimp about halfway through. Do not remove the shell. Remove the vein with the nose of the scissors and pull off the legs. Rinse the shrimp under cold running water, drain in a colander, and pat dry.

3. Preheat a skillet over high heat. Add 2½ tablespoons of the oil, then add the shrimp and stir-fry until the shrimp are almost cooked through, about 5 minutes. They will

be charred and deep orange in color. Transfer the shrimp to a bowl or plate.

4. Return the skillet to high heat and add the remaining 2 teaspoons oil. Add the scallions, ginger, and garlic, and stir-fry until fragrant, about 30 seconds. Stir the seasoning sauce to recombine and add it all at once to the skillet, stirring until the sauce thickens slightly.

5. Return the shrimp to the skillet and stir until they are evenly coated with the sauce. Remove from the heat and swirl in the sesame oil. Serve hot.

Tuna Burgers

SERVES 4

◆ EXTRA-QUICK

1 SMALL RED ONION, QUARTERED

1 CELERY RIB, QUARTERED

TWO 6½-OUNCE CANS WATER-PACKED
SOLID WHITE TUNA, WELL DRAINED

1 EGG

3 SLICES WHOLE WHEAT OR WHITE
BREAD, TORN INTO PIECES

2 TABLESPOONS UNSALTED BUTTER

2 TEASPOONS DIJON MUSTARD

¼ TEASPOON CAYENNE PEPPER

¼ TEASPOON BLACK PEPPER

¼ CUP FLOUR

2 TABLESPOONS OLIVE OIL

1. Place the onion and celery in a food processor and pulse the machine on and off to coarsely chop. Add the tuna and process briefly to break it up.

2. Add the egg, bread, butter, mustard, cayenne, and black pepper, and process until just blended.

3. Place the flour in a shallow bowl. Lightly flour your hands and shape the tuna mixture into 4 patties about 4 inches across. Dredge the patties lightly in the flour.

4. In a large skillet, preferably nonstick, warm the oil over medium-high heat. Add the patties and cook until browned, about 3 minutes on each side. Serve hot.

Variation: *If you're tired of tuna, try using canned salmon instead. Use two small cans or one large can and drain very well. To highlight the salmon's richer flavor, add some grated lemon zest and a few drops of lemon juice to the burger mixture.*

CRISPY FLOUNDER
WITH SWEET-AND-SOUR SAUCE

SERVES 4

½ CUP PLAIN LOW-FAT YOGURT
1 TABLESPOON APRICOT JAM OR
    ORANGE MARMALADE
2 TEASPOONS DIJON MUSTARD
1 TEASPOON CIDER VINEGAR
1 TABLESPOON CHOPPED PARSLEY
    (OPTIONAL)
1 EGG

2 TABLESPOONS MILK
¾ CUP FINE UNSEASONED DRY BREAD
    CRUMBS
¼ CUP GRATED PARMESAN CHEESE
½ TEASPOON SALT
¼ TEASPOON BLACK PEPPER
1½ POUNDS FLOUNDER, SOLE, OR SEA
    BASS FILLETS (½ INCH THICK)

1. In a medium bowl, combine the yogurt, apricot jam, mustard, vinegar, and parsley (if using). Stir to blend.

2. Preheat the oven to 400°. Line a baking sheet with foil and lightly oil the foil.

3. In a shallow bowl, beat the egg and milk together. In another shallow bowl or platter, combine the bread crumbs, Parmesan, salt, and pepper. Dip the fish first into the egg mixture and then into the bread crumb mixture, coating well on both sides.

4. Place the fish on the prepared baking sheet in a single layer. Bake, uncovered, for 10 to 12 minutes, or until the fish is opaque and just flakes when tested with a fork.

5. Serve the fish hot with the sweet-and-sour sauce on the side.

Broiled Sole with Garlic Butter and Bread Crumbs

SERVES 4

◆ EXTRA-QUICK

2 TABLESPOONS OLIVE OIL

2 TABLESPOONS UNSALTED BUTTER

3 GARLIC CLOVES, MINCED

4 SOLE FILLETS (ABOUT 1½ POUNDS
   TOTAL)

2 TEASPOONS GRATED LEMON ZEST

2 TABLESPOONS DIJON MUSTARD

¼ CUP CHOPPED PARSLEY

1 TEASPOON OREGANO

¼ TEASPOON SALT

¼ TEASPOON BLACK PEPPER

3 TABLESPOONS FRESH LEMON JUICE

¼ CUP FINE UNSEASONED DRY BREAD
   CRUMBS

1. Preheat the broiler.

2. In a large broilerproof skillet, warm the oil with the butter over medium heat until the butter is melted. Add the garlic and cook, stirring occasionally, until the garlic is fragrant and light golden, about 3 minutes.

3. Measure out 2 tablespoons of the garlic butter and set aside in a small bowl. Increase the heat under the skillet to medium-high. Add the fish and cook until golden brown on the bottom, about 4 minutes. Remove the skillet from the heat.

4. Meanwhile, in a small bowl, combine the lemon zest, mustard, 2 tablespoons of the parsley, the oregano, salt, and pepper.

5. Sprinkle the lemon juice over the fish in the skillet. Spread the mustard mixture over the fish and then dust with the bread crumbs. Drizzle the reserved garlic butter on top.

6. Place the skillet under the broiler and broil 4 inches from the heat until the top is golden and the fish just flakes when tested with a fork, about 3 minutes.

7. Sprinkle with the remaining parsley and serve hot.

Spicy Broiled Salmon

SERVES 4

¼ CUP ORANGE JUICE

2 TABLESPOONS DRY VERMOUTH OR
DRY WHITE WINE

2 TABLESPOONS FRESH LIME JUICE

1 FRESH OR PICKLED JALAPEÑO PEPPER,
SEEDED AND FINELY CHOPPED

1 GARLIC CLOVE, MINCED

1 TEASPOON FRESH THYME, OR
¼ TEASPOON DRIED

⅛ TEASPOON ALLSPICE

4 SALMON FILLETS, WITH SKIN (ABOUT
1½ POUNDS TOTAL)

1½ TABLESPOONS UNSALTED BUTTER,
CUT INTO SMALL PIECES

1. In a small bowl, combine the orange juice, vermouth, lime juice, jalapeño pepper, garlic, thyme, and allspice. Place the fillets in an ovenproof dish and pour the marinade over them. Let the fillets marinate at room temperature for 15 minutes. Preheat the broiler.

2. Strain and reserve the marinade. Broil the fish about 4 inches from the heat, basting every 3 minutes with the marinade, for 10 to 12 minutes, or until the fish just flakes when tested with a fork.

3. Scatter the butter over the top, return the fillets to the broiler, and cook them a few seconds to melt the butter. Serve hot.

Sweet Afterthought: *Peel 4 navel oranges, using a sharp knife to remove all the white pith (work over a bowl to catch the juice). Slice the oranges crosswise about ¼ inch thick and layer the slices in a shallow glass dish, sprinkling a little granulated sugar over each layer. Pour in the reserved juice, then add enough sherry to cover the oranges. Chill for at least 4 hours and serve ice cold.*

BROILED SWORDFISH WITH HERB BUTTER

SERVES 4

1 STICK UNSALTED BUTTER

1 GARLIC CLOVE, MINCED

2 TABLESPOONS FRESH LEMON JUICE

1 TABLESPOON FRESH LIME JUICE

¼ CUP MIXED CHOPPED FRESH HERBS
(SEE KITCHEN NOTE, BELOW)

4 SWORDFISH STEAKS (1 INCH THICK,
ABOUT 2 POUNDS TOTAL)

2 TABLESPOONS OLIVE OIL

1. In a food processor or blender, combine the butter, garlic, lemon juice, lime juice, and mixed herbs, and process until well blended. Form the herb butter into a log-shaped roll 2 inches long and 2 to 2½ inches in diameter. Wrap snugly in wax paper and place in the freezer for 1 hour or refrigerate for several hours.

2. Preheat the broiler and broiler pan.

3. Lightly brush both sides of the steaks with the oil. Place the steaks on the preheated broiler pan and broil for 4 to 5 minutes. Turn and broil for 2 to 3 minutes, or until opaque throughout.

4. Cut the herb butter into 1 or 2 generous slices for each steak. Top the steaks with the butter and broil for 1 minute, or just until the butter begins to melt.

KITCHEN NOTE: *The herbs used here can vary widely with availability or your preference. Use any combination of watercress, parsley, dill, basil, and rosemary. Make at least half of the mixture one of the fleshier, greener herbs, such as watercress or parsley. And when using rosemary, be somewhat conservative—no more than one-eighth of the total—as it is a strongly flavored herb.*

Parmesan Scallop Gratin

SERVES 4

◆ EXTRA-QUICK

1 CUP CHICKEN BROTH, PREFERABLY
  REDUCED-SODIUM
¼ TEASPOON NUTMEG
¼ TEASPOON PEPPER, PREFERABLY
  WHITE
1 POUND SEA SCALLOPS
2 TABLESPOONS UNSALTED BUTTER
1 TABLESPOON FLOUR

¼ CUP HEAVY CREAM
2 TABLESPOONS GRATED PARMESAN
  CHEESE
1 TABLESPOON SEASONED DRY BREAD
  CRUMBS
2 TABLESPOONS CHOPPED PARSLEY
  (OPTIONAL)

1. In a medium saucepan, bring the chicken broth, nutmeg, and pepper to a boil over medium-high heat. Add the scallops and let the mixture return to a boil. Reduce the heat to low, cover, and simmer until the scallops are barely cooked, about 3 minutes. With a slotted spoon, transfer the scallops to a bowl and cover loosely with foil to keep warm. Reserve the cooking liquid.

2. Preheat the broiler.

3. In a small saucepan, warm 1 tablespoon of the butter over medium heat until melted. Stir in the flour and cook, stirring, until the flour is no longer visible, about 15 seconds.

Add the cream and ¼ cup of the reserved cooking liquid. Cook, stirring, until the mixture just starts to simmer and thicken, about 2 minutes. (If the sauce seems too thick, add a bit more cooking liquid.)

4. Combine the sauce and scallops, and toss to coat. Turn the mixture into a 1-quart gratin dish or shallow baking dish. Sprinkle with the Parmesan and bread crumbs, and dot with the remaining 1 tablespoon butter. Broil 4 inches from the heat until golden on top, 2 to 4 minutes. Garnish with the parsley, if desired.

Garlic-Lemon Shrimp

SERVES 4

3 TABLESPOONS UNSALTED BUTTER

¼ CUP (PACKED) FRESH DILL SPRIGS, MINCED, OR 2 TEASPOONS DRIED

3 SCALLIONS, FINELY CHOPPED

3 GARLIC CLOVES, MINCED

1 TABLESPOON GRATED LEMON ZEST

¼ TEASPOON SALT

¼ TEASPOON BLACK PEPPER

½ CUP FRESH LEMON JUICE

1 POUND MEDIUM SHRIMP

2 TEASPOONS FLOUR

1. Preheat the broiler or prepare the grill. If broiling, line a broiler pan with foil.

2. In a small saucepan, warm 2 tablespoons of the butter over medium heat until melted. Add the dill, scallions, garlic, lemon zest, salt, and pepper. Stir in the lemon juice.

3. If desired, shell and devein the shrimp. Thread the shrimp on skewers (if broiling, place the skewers on the broiler pan) and brush them with some of the garlic-lemon basting mixture.

4. Grill or broil the shrimp 4 inches from the heat until they begin to turn pink, 2 to 3 minutes. Turn the shrimp over, brush with some more basting mixture and broil until the shrimp are cooked through, 2 to 3 minutes.

5. Meanwhile, thoroughly blend the remaining 1 tablespoon butter with the flour. Return the remaining basting mixture to medium-high heat and bring to a boil. Add the butter-flour mixture bit by bit, stirring well after each addition, and cook until the sauce has thickened slightly, 2 to 3 minutes.

6. Serve the shrimp with the sauce on the side.

PAELLA SALAD

SERVES 4

2 CUPS CHICKEN BROTH, PREFERABLY REDUCED-SODIUM

2 GARLIC CLOVES, MINCED

2 TEASPOONS TURMERIC

½ TEASPOON BLACK PEPPER

1 CUP RICE

¾ POUND MEDIUM SHRIMP—SHELLED, DEVEINED, AND CUT INTO BITE-SIZE PIECES

¼ POUND UNSLICED HAM, CUT INTO ½-INCH CUBES

1 LARGE GREEN BELL PEPPER, CUT INTO THIN STRIPS

1 MEDIUM RED BELL PEPPER, COARSELY CHOPPED

1 MEDIUM RED ONION, CUT INTO THIN RINGS

¼ CUP CHOPPED PARSLEY (OPTIONAL)

3 TABLESPOONS OLIVE OIL

2 TABLESPOONS FRESH LEMON JUICE

1¼ TEASPOONS GRATED LEMON ZEST

1. In a large skillet, bring the chicken broth, garlic, turmeric, and black pepper to a boil over medium-high heat. Add the rice, reduce the heat to medium-low, cover, and simmer for 15 minutes.

2. Add the shrimp to the rice and cook for 5 minutes, or until the shrimp are cooked through and the rice is tender.

3. Remove the rice from the heat and stir in the ham, bell peppers, onion, parsley (if using), oil, lemon juice, and lemon zest.

4. Serve warm, at room temperature, or chilled.

SUBSTITUTION: *For a more authentic Spanish flavor, use ½ teaspoon of crumbled saffron threads instead of the turmeric. Saffron is expensive, but a little goes a long way.*

Index

Recipes that are marked in the body of the book with the symbol ◆ take 30 minutes or less to prepare. They are grouped in the index under the name Extra-Quick. Recipes that are marked in the body of the book with the symbol ◇ derive 30% or fewer of their calories from fat. They are grouped in the index under the name Low-Fat.

A-B

Asian Crab-and-Vegetable Salad, 110
Blackened Seafood Stew, 26
Boston Crab Chowder with Nutmeg Croutons, 17
Brook Trout with Mushroom Sauce, 59
Burgers, Tuna, 118

C

Caribbean Red Snapper Stew, 22
Chinese-Style Poached Fish Fillets, 35
Chowder
 Boston Crab Chowder with Nutmeg Croutons, 17
 Fast Fish Chowder, 12
 Mixed Seafood Chowder, 111
 New England Fish Chowder, 15
 Rich Red Snapper Chowder with Carrots, 14
 Salmon and Corn Chowder, 13
 Tomato-Clam Chowder with Garlic Toasts, 16
Cioppino, Quick, with Parsley Toasts, 25
Clams
 Savory Clam and Rice Soup, 8
 Seafood Soup Provençale, 7
 Tomato-Clam Chowder with Garlic Toasts, 16
Cod
 Baked Cod with Tomatoes and Provolone, 71
 Cod Basque-Style, 37
 Cod Steaks Topped with Tomato and Basil, 94
 Cod Stewed with Potatoes, Corn, and Tomatoes, 24
 Codfish Cakes with Horseradish Sauce, 69
 Fast Fish Chowder, 12
 Fish Curry with Spinach and Peanuts, 19
 Fish Soup with Vegetables and Red Pepper Sauce, 6

Grilled Fish Salad, 104
Mixed Seafood Chowder, 111
New England Fish Chowder, 15
New Orleans Fish and Oyster Stew, 27
Oriental Oven-Steamed Fish with Vegetables, 33
Seafood Soup Provençale, 7
Shallow-Fried Fish Tempura with Two Sauces, 47
Crab
 Asian Crab-and-Vegetable Salad, 110
 Boston Crab Chowder with Nutmeg Croutons, 17
 Broiled Crab-Potato Patties, 103
 Crab Cakes with Quick Rémoulade Sauce, 61
 Light Seafood Newburg, 112
 Quick Cioppino with Parsley Toasts, 25
 Steamed Spiced Crabs, 114
Creole-Style Scallops and Rice, 29
Curry/curried food
 Curried Flounder with Mushrooms, 21
 Fish Curry with Spinach and Peanuts, 19
 Sautéed Curried Grouper, 48
 Shrimp Curry with Coconut-Almond Rice, 31

E-F

Extra-Quick
 Beer Batter Fillets with Red Pepper Slaw, 116
 Bourbon-Basted Salmon, 83
 Broiled Sole with Garlic Butter and Bread Crumbs, 120
 Corn, Scallop, and Fettuccine Soup, 11
 Corn-Fried Snapper with Spicy Pineapple Salsa, 53
 Crab Cakes with Quick Rémoulade Sauce, 61
 Fast Fish Chowder, 12
 Fish Curry with Spinach and Peanuts, 19
 Flounder with Lemon Cream, 90
 Grilled Fish Salad, 104
 Herb-Coated Salmon, 84
 Lemon Scallops with Green Beans, 62
 Parmesan Scallop Gratin, 123
 Pecan-Crusted Snapper with Scallions, 54

Red Snapper with Spicy Orange Sauce, 56
Salmon with Dill Sauce, 41
Sautéed Curried Grouper, 48
Sautéed Sesame Fish, 46
Scallop-Mushroom Noodle Soup, 9
Steamed Fish with Ginger, Scallions, and Cilantro, 34
Swordfish Piccata, 60
Tex-Mex Steamed Swordfish, 42
Tomato-Clam Chowder with Garlic Toasts, 16
Tuna Burgers, 118
Tuna-Spinach Salad with Peanut Dressing, 107
Zesty Tuna with Mexican Seasonings, 106
Flounder
 Baked Tarragon Fish, 68
 Beer Batter Fillets with Red Pepper Slaw, 116
 Breaded Fish with Lemon Butter, 45
 Chinese-Style Poached Fish Fillets, 35
 Crispy Flounder with Sweet-and-Sour Sauce, 119
 Curried Flounder with Mushrooms, 21
 Fillets of Flounder Capri, 36
 Fillets of Flounder Sorrento, 72
 Flounder Rolls Stuffed with Cheese and Spinach, 70
 Flounder with Lemon Cream, 90
 Shrimp-Stuffed Baked Fish, 73
 Skillet-Baked Flounder Provençale, 75

G-H

Gratin, Parmesan Scallop, 123
Greek-Style Baked Haddock, 74
Grilled/broiled dishes
 Broiled Crab-Potato Patties, 103
 Broiled Salmon with Green Sauce, 96
 Broiled Scrod with Red Pepper Butter, 92
 Broiled Shrimp with Cilantro-Citrus Butter, 102
 Broiled Sole with Garlic Butter and Bread Crumbs, 120
 Broiled Swordfish with Herb Butter, 122
 Broiled Tuna with Orange-Cumin Sauce, 99
 Cod Steaks Topped with Tomato and Basil, 94
 Flounder with Lemon Cream, 90

Garlic-Lemon Shrimp, 124
Grilled Fish Salad, 104
Grilled Salmon Steaks with Fresh Dill
  and Thyme, 95
Grilled Shrimp with Tomato-Ginger
  Sauce, 101
Lemon-Marinated Swordfish Kebabs,
  97
Lime-Dressed Snapper with Potatoes
  and Peppers, 91
Marinated Red Snapper, 93
Parmesan Scallop Gratin, 123
Scallop and Vegetable Skewers with
  Garlic Butter, 100
Spicy Broiled Salmon, 121
Swordfish with Spicy Tomato-Orange
  Sauce, 98
Grouper
  Mixed Seafood Chowder, 111
  Mushroom-Smothered Baked Fish, 76
  Sautéed Curried Grouper, 48
  Seafood Stew with Water Chestnuts,
    23
  Shallow-Fried Fish Tempura with Two
    Sauces, 47
Haddock
  Fast Fish Chowder, 12
  Fish Curry with Spinach and Peanuts,
    19
  Fish Soup with Vegetables and Red
    Pepper Sauce, 6
  Greek-Style Baked Haddock, 74
  Italian-Style Fish Fillets, 18
  New England Fish Chowder, 15
  Pan-Fried Haddock with Spanish
    Vegetables, 49
Halibut
  Buttermilk Baked Halibut, 77
  Grilled Fish Salad, 104
  Mixed Seafood Chowder, 111
  New Orleans Fish and Oyster Stew,
    27
  Pan-Fried Halibut with Sweet-and-
    Sour Sauce, 44
  Sautéed Sesame Fish, 46
  Seafood Soup Provençale, 7
  Steamed Fish with Ginger, Scallions,
    and Cilantro, 34

I-L

Italian-Style Fish Fillets, 18
Kebabs
  Grilled Shrimp with Tomato-Ginger
    Sauce, 101
  Lemon-Marinated Swordfish Kebabs,
    97
  Scallop and Vegetable Skewers with
    Garlic Butter, 100

Low-Fat
  Caribbean Red Snapper Stew, 22
  Cod Steaks Topped with Tomato and
    Basil, 94
  Cod Stewed with Potatoes, Corn, and
    Tomatoes, 24
  Corn, Scallop, and Fettuccine Soup,
    11
  Creole-Style Scallops and Rice, 29
  Curried Flounder with Mushrooms,
    21
  Fast Fish Chowder, 12
  Flounder Rolls Stuffed with Cheese
    and Spinach, 70
  Greek-Style Baked Haddock, 74
  Italian-Style Fish Fillets, 18
  Lemon Scallops with Green Beans,
    62
  Oriental Oven-Steamed Fish with
    Vegetables, 33
  Salmon and Corn Chowder, 13
  Sautéed Curried Grouper, 48
  Sautéed Shrimp with Sherry and
    Chilies, 66
  Savory Clam and Rice Soup, 8
  Scallop-Asparagus Stir-Fry with
    Curried Rice, 63
  Scallop-Mushroom Noodle Soup, 9
  Seafood Stew with Water Chestnuts,
    23
  Steamed Spiced Crabs, 114
  Swordfish and Leeks with Bell Pepper
    Purée, 43
  Tex-Mex Steamed Swordfish, 42
  Tomato-Clam Chowder with Garlic
    Toasts, 16
  Zesty Tuna with Mexican Seasonings,
    106

M-O

Mexican-Style Shrimp with Pasta and
  Tomatoes, 30
Mexican-Style Sole with Almonds, 57
Monkfish Provençale, 50
Mussels
  Mussels Marinière, 113
  Seafood Soup Provençale, 7
New England Fish Chowder, 15
Ocean perch
  Blackened Seafood Stew, 26
  Fish Soup with Vegetables and Red
    Pepper Sauce, 6
  Mushroom-Smothered Baked Fish, 76
  New England Fish Chowder, 15
Oriental Oven-Steamed Fish with
  Vegetables, 33
Oysters
  New Orleans Fish and Oyster Stew, 27

P-R

Paella Salad, 125
Poached/steamed dishes
  Chinese-Style Poached Fish Fillets, 35
  Cod Basque-Style, 37
  Fillets of Flounder Capri, 36
  Oriental Oven-Steamed Fish with
    Vegetables, 33
  Poached Salmon in Orange-Lemon
    Sauce, 38
  Poached Salmon with Dill Butter, 40
  Red Snapper with Vegetable Julienne,
    39
  Salmon with Dill Sauce, 41
  Steamed Fish with Ginger, Scallions,
    and Cilantro, 34
  Steamed Spiced Crabs, 114
  Swordfish and Leeks with Bell Pepper
    Purée, 43
  Tex-Mex Steamed Swordfish, 42
Red snapper
  Baked Red Snapper with Chili Sauce,
    85
  Blackened Seafood Stew, 26
  Caribbean Red Snapper Stew, 22
  Corn-Fried Snapper with Spicy
    Pineapple Salsa, 53
  Lime-Dressed Snapper with Potatoes
    and Peppers, 91
  Marinated Red Snapper, 93
  Mushroom-Smothered Baked Fish, 76
  Oriental Oven-Steamed Fish with
    Vegetables, 33
  Pan-Blackened Red Snapper, 115
  Pecan-Crusted Snapper with Scallions,
    54
  Quick Cioppino with Parsley Toasts,
    25
  Red Snapper with Spicy Orange Sauce,
    56
  Red Snapper with Toasted Almonds,
    55
  Red Snapper with Vegetable Julienne,
    39
  Rich Red Snapper Chowder with
    Carrots, 14
  Sautéed Sesame Fish, 46
  Seafood Stew with Water Chestnuts,
    23
  Spicy Fish Ragout over Lemon Rice,
    20
  Steamed Fish with Ginger, Scallions,
    and Cilantro, 34

S

Salads, main-course
  Asian Crab-and-Vegetable Salad, 110
  Grilled Fish Salad, 104

Paella Salad, 125
Salmon-Rice Salad with Lemon-Pepper Dressing, 105
Shrimp and Green Bean Salad, 109
Tuna Salad Niçoise, 108
Tuna-Spinach Salad with Peanut Dressing, 107
Zesty Tuna with Mexican Seasonings, 106
Salmon
Bourbon-Basted Salmon, 83
Broiled Salmon with Green Sauce, 96
Grilled Salmon Steaks with Fresh Dill and Thyme, 95
Herb-Coated Salmon, 84
Poached Salmon in Orange-Lemon Sauce, 38
Poached Salmon with Dill Butter, 40
Salmon and Corn Chowder, 13
Salmon Patties with Citrus Vinaigrette, 51
Salmon with Dill Sauce, 41
Salmon with Fresh Basil Sauce, 52
Salmon-Rice Salad with Lemon-Pepper Dressing, 105
Spicy Broiled Salmon, 121
Scallops
Corn, Scallop, and Fettuccine Soup, 11
Creole-Style Scallops and Rice, 29
Lemon Scallops with Green Beans, 62
Light Seafood Newburg, 112
Parmesan Scallop Gratin, 123
Ragout of Scallops and Red Peppers, 28
Scallop and Vegetable Skewers with Garlic Butter, 100
Scallop-Asparagus Stir-Fry with Curried Rice, 63
Scallop-Mushroom Noodle Soup, 9
Scrod, Broiled, with Red Pepper Butter, 92
Sea bass
Italian-Style Fish Fillets, 18
Oriental Oven-Steamed Fish with Vegetables, 33
Sautéed Sesame Fish, 46
Seafood Soup Provençale, 7
Spicy Fish Ragout over Lemon Rice, 20
Steamed Fish with Ginger, Scallions, and Cilantro, 34
Shrimp
Baked Stuffed Shrimp with Tomato Tartar Sauce, 89
Blackened Seafood Stew, 26

Broiled Shrimp with Cilantro-Citrus Butter, 102
Chili Shrimp, 117
Garlic Shrimp with Cuban Black Bean Salad, 67
Garlic-Lemon Shrimp, 124
Grilled Shrimp with Tomato-Ginger Sauce, 101
Lemon-Garlic Shrimp with Parslied Rice, 65
Light Seafood Newburg, 112
Mexican-Style Shrimp with Pasta and Tomatoes, 30
Mixed Seafood Chowder, 111
Paella Salad, 125
Sautéed Shrimp with Sherry and Chilies, 66
Seafood Soup Provençale, 7
Seafood Stew with Water Chestnuts, 23
Shrimp and Green Bean Salad, 109
Shrimp Curry with Coconut-Almond Rice, 31
Shrimp with Green Chili Creole Sauce, 32
Shrimp-Stuffed Baked Fish, 73
Spicy Shrimp and Spinach Soup, 10
Spicy Shrimp on Zucchini Nests, 64
Sole
Baked Sole with Mushrooms and Tomatoes, 80
Baked Sole with Zucchini and Peppers, 81
Baked Tarragon Fish, 68
Beer Batter Fillets with Red Pepper Slaw, 116
Breaded Fish with Lemon Butter, 45
Broiled Sole with Garlic Butter and Bread Crumbs, 120
Chinese-Style Poached Fish Fillets, 35
Fillets of Sole in Wine Sauce, 79
Foil-Baked Sole and Vegetables with Herb Butter, 82
Mexican-Style Sole with Almonds, 57
Shrimp-Stuffed Baked Fish, 73
Sole Baked in Parchment, 78
Sole with Tomato-Basil Sauce, 58
Soups. See also Chowder
Corn, Scallop, and Fettuccine Soup, 11
Fish Soup with Vegetables and Red Pepper Sauce, 6
Savory Clam and Rice Soup, 8
Scallop-Mushroom Noodle Soup, 9
Seafood Soup Provençale, 7
Spicy Shrimp and Spinach Soup, 10
Stews

Blackened Seafood Stew, 26
Caribbean Red Snapper Stew, 22
Cod Stewed with Potatoes, Corn, and Tomatoes, 24
Fish Curry with Spinach and Peanuts, 19
Light Seafood Newburg, 112
New Orleans Fish and Oyster Stew, 27
Quick Cioppino with Parsley Toasts, 25
Ragout of Scallops and Red Peppers, 28
Seafood Stew with Water Chestnuts, 23
Shrimp Curry with Coconut-Almond Rice, 31
Spicy Fish Ragout over Lemon Rice, 20
Striped bass
Quick Cioppino with Parsley Toasts, 25
Striped Bass with Fennel and Romaine, 87
Swordfish
Broiled Swordfish with Herb Butter, 122
Lemon-Marinated Swordfish Kebabs, 97
New Orleans Fish and Oyster Stew, 27
Swordfish and Leeks with Bell Pepper Purée, 43
Swordfish Piccata, 60
Swordfish with Spicy Tomato-Orange Sauce, 98
Tex-Mex Steamed Swordfish, 42

T

Tex-Mex Steamed Swordfish, 42
Trout
Brook Trout with Mushroom Sauce, 59
Skillet-Baked Trout with Lemon-Caper Sauce, 86
Tuna
Broiled Tuna with Orange-Cumin Sauce, 99
Tuna Baked in Parchment with Red Peppers, 88
Tuna Burgers, 118
Tuna Salad Niçoise, 108
Tuna-Spinach Salad with Peanut Dressing, 107
Zesty Tuna with Mexican Seasonings, 106